NOTHING TO PROVE

NOTHING TO PROVE

LEE SCHRANER

For my dearest Mum, Sally Schraner

Front Cover: Caricature artwork by James Brennan
Proof Read & Edited by Bradleigh Griffiths

CHAPTER 1

Genius

Ctrl-Alt-Del and life began.

I may have been just five years old, but to hear your Prep teacher tell mum that I was a 'genius' was something I will never forget.

Facemaker was the program I was on. Building your own personal characters on a green screen in 1987 was about as advanced as computer technology had come. I had a fascination for big noses and older people, even at that age, and was always creating a similar character.

My three-key hit was something I had seen before. With a flying brain and extensive memory already, repeating what I had seen was not a difficult task. I was in the back end of the computer and knew a few prompt codes. By typing 'list', the whole program code appeared, giving me access to every line of code used to build Facemaker.

Obviously at that age I had no idea about computer code. It took a minute or two for the thousands of lines of computer language to appear on the screen. Once it stopped, I simply typed 'print' to get a hard copy of the code. The dot matrix printer started its laborious shriek as it inked each line onto the tractor-feed paper, alerting classmates and my teacher.

My teacher was in hysterics. She was so furious that she grabbed me by the arm and dragged me straight to the principal's office. Technology was a pretty scary thing in the mid-1980's and she was certain I had purposely broken the computer and printer.

She telephoned my mum and ordered her straight to the school, telling her that I had destroyed a computer and printer and that if it couldn't be fixed, mum was going to have to cough up the dollars for replacements. You could imagine mum freaking out on her drive to school. How could my mum possibly afford to pay for an expensive computer and printer?

Fair to say I was aware of the situation, but not concerned in the slightest. I knew what I had done and my principal and teacher just didn't understand. It was pretty funny listening to her preach to the principal about the damage I had caused. So much so, that I got in even more trouble giggling at her panic.

By the time mum arrived, our school I.T. worker had re-booted the computer and returned it to its normal state. The printer had paused part-way through the code and fed to the next perforated tear line. He explained to my mum, teacher, and principal what I had done. A child my age was not supposed to be able to spell those words, let alone know computer short codes. Yet, I was able to execute them in the correct order to get exactly what I wanted out of the system.

My teacher apologised profusely to mum, telling her that it was a simple misunderstanding. In 15 minutes, she had done a complete backflip from her earlier song and dance.

A discussion took place with all involved. I sat in the chair minding my own business and taking it all in. It was during that conversation my teacher hinted I was possibly a 'genius' for my age. Just a few minutes earlier mum was worried about finding money to repair a computer and now she was being told her mudpie eating toddler might be a genius. Imagine the emotional roller-coaster!

1987 technology compared to the current day was laughable. The VCR was the greatest invention of the era, the car phone was top dollar, and the internet was still almost three years away from initial use at Melbourne University. This is probably why my teacher was in awe of what I had done. Breaking into the back end of a program and being able to change the code to anything I wanted (not that I had any idea how to write code) was a big deal then.

The following couple of months at school felt distant. I knew things were a little bit different with the other kids, but being my first year of school, it seemed normal enough to me. It makes a lot more sense to me today than it did at the time. Often, I was pulled out of the classroom away from my friends and peers, subjected to tasks that no-one else was asked to do.

From memory, I did things like an Australian weather report on camera, being able to name all Capital cities and improvise the commentary to go with each temperature forecast. I was given books to read aloud that included topics and words much longer than any five-year-old should be reading. I learnt long division, large sum multiplications and basic trigonometry. I knew who Pythagoras was at three feet tall.

I was asked to solve puzzles and riddles either cold-turkey or by reading instructions. I never solved them all, but certainly got through more than was expected. I was even given an Atlas to study and tested on Australian and world geography.

In my teenage years, mum finally told me the truth. Little to my knowledge at the time, she had knocked back serious offers from places such as the 'Krongold Centre for gifted children' and many others. Mum didn't want me to be isolated from my friends, subjected to tests and experiments, and studied by medical professionals. I wonder if she ever knew what the school put me through that year. I guarantee she was never told about the closed-door testing.

No matter how 'gifted' or intelligent these people thought I was, mum was convinced that the best thing for me was to grow up as a normal kid. It must have been one hell of a decision to make about her eldest child, but a decision I will forever be grateful for. Being a spoilt brat who thought they were better than everyone else, is not something I would have been proud of.

I was brought up with both feet on the ground. A stable base would put me in good stead for the rest of my life. I was taught to be humble, protective, and helpful. I could use my skills to help struggling friends through school and make life a little bit easier for them, rather than sitting back and looking at their blank stares of misunderstanding. I had a lot of good friends who would return the favour by looking out for their 'little' mate and keeping the bullies away from making fun of me. This was more than just an arrangement; this was what friendship was all about. We all had our strengths, and together we would form an impenetrable bond that would get us through our first year of school.

And I still ate mud pies.

CHAPTER 2

Firefly

My father had taken his love of alcohol too far.

As he passed out in the armchair, mum quietly got the attention of me and my younger sister. You could appreciate the whiteness and alertness in her eyes as she ushered us to our bedroom with her index finger firmly placed on her lips. Her tremble was obvious.

She began throwing our clothes into suitcases one-handed, being sure to keep her finger pressed at her lips. We may have been young, but we both knew to keep quiet.

We weren't leaving, we were fleeing. Whether it was planned or not, I'll never know. Quite simply I never asked. This wasn't ever talked about again.

In evening darkness at the Spencer Street Station bus terminal, our family of three along with mum's friend Lisa, all boarded a

Firefly bus headed for Sydney. We left with little more than the clothes on our back.

The bus driver was a spitting image of Ian Turpie. Being a young game show enthusiast, all I could think about was 'Whammies' and 'Big Bucks' from my favourite television show 'Press Your Luck'. This guy, however, didn't seem as pleasant as Ian Turpie. He was very sly and unappealing, which only creeped me out more when he started flirting with my mum. Despite having two young children, one in each hand, this guy only had his own interests at heart. The trip up the Hume Highway was sure to be long and uncomfortable.

I must have slept through most of the late evening and early morning, only to be awoken by the bus braking, as we pulled into the Big Merino at Goulburn. It must have been around 3:00am in the morning, but it was time for an early breakfast. Unsurprisingly, our bus driver 'friend' had ordered and made his way to our table. I vividly recall people eating tin spaghetti on toast, sandwiches, and fried eggs, with most having some sort of coffee or tea steaming from their table. Bus trips of this length can be very exhausting, even if you do sit down for the whole journey.

A couple of hours down the road, we stopped at Liverpool to let some passengers off. Mum made a spontaneous decision to end our trip there, even though our tickets were paid to Sydney. She was a clever lady my mum. By cutting our journey short, she knew we would be separated from any further attention from our 'Big

Bucks' buddy. He had no option but to drive the bus on to Sydney, allowing us to disappear into the cold Liverpool night.

We didn't walk far before we came across a small caravan park. This would be a great little place to spend a few days on a tight budget. By this time, it was still pitch black and not even 6:00am in the morning. Reception was strangely manned, albeit by a toothless, rugged old man. There were no vans available until the morning, so we were treated with tales of the park and stale biscuits until the sun finally woke from its slumber. That morning sun had never looked so good.

The van we were given was a disgrace. Mum refused to let either of us kids go inside until she had given it a complete top to bottom scrub. It wasn't just the dust, it was the dozens of cockroaches, maggots, and other creepy crawlies that were infesting the caravan.

It was a wet morning and me and my sister had found an awesome mud pit. We were covered head to toe in a black mess, shivering from the morning rain. I wonder what mum was thinking when she spotted us in that state. Maybe she was just happy to see that we were having a good time and playing together as though we were in our own front yard back in Melbourne. Either way, we were eventually marched to the communal showers to be scrubbed clean.

Later that afternoon, mum had picked up some groceries and was looking to get some dinner on the stove. We always ate early, generally around 5:00pm. The stove in the caravan wouldn't light and mum wasn't even sure if the gas was hooked up correctly. Maybe a neighbouring van could help.

A young Maltese man in the small van next to us was more than happy to help. I'm not sure at the time if he was being a local gentleman, or if he too had the same interests as the bus driver and the park receptionist. In any event, he got the stove working and we were able to have a home-cooked meal for dinner.

If I remember right, mum invited the man for dinner, and we ate as a five. It was us two kids, mum, Lisa, and mum's new friend. I suppose it was convenient to befriend a local man who could help us out, and even protect us from any unwanted trouble in the park. Liverpool wasn't a great area in the mid-to-late 1980's and even today, many people choose to avoid walking the streets after dark.

The young Maltese man claimed to be 21 and told us his name was Martin. He gloated about his omelette recipe and promised to cook them for us the next morning. Mum placed a lot of trust in him and allowed him to visit the next day and cook us breakfast. He was right. Those omelettes were magnificent.

Call it fate if you will, but let the story be told. Martin Schraner married my mum three years later in 1990, and along came my two younger brothers, Beau, and Mathew. Funnily, the first-time mum saw Martin's real age was in the wedding papers. He was a couple of days shy of 21, meaning he was just 18 when mum first met him. It was a well-hidden lie.

The marriage would last more than 25 years before they separated. Martin became affectionately known as dad or 'papa' to me, and even though he and mum are no longer one, the family remains civil and friendly during the holiday period, birthdays, and other family occasions.

I assumed the Schraner surname in the early 1990's and had it changed by deed poll the day I turned 18. It was my 18th birthday wish that my surname become official in the eyes of the law.

Lee Peterson was no more.

CHAPTER 3

Woolombumbuck

The Woolombumbuck star was the brightest star in the sky.

The star was always first to appear when the sun went down. It shone brightly on the Woolombumbuck tree, where inside lived the Woolombumbuck babies. Only when the star sparkled in the night sky, could the Woolombumbuck babies lay their weary heads to sleep.

Martin had some fantastic bedtime stories. This one though, was the most memorable. I'm not sure how many times we sat outside the caravan waiting eagerly for the Woolombumbuck star to appear. The poor Woolombumbuck babies couldn't rest until it did, and neither could me or my sister. The story was a classic; a fraud nonetheless, but it ignited my imagination most every night. Martin was making sure my sister and I would sleep easy. Once in the land of nod, he and mum would have time to themselves.

The morning would come and as usual, I would be the first one awake. Sometimes it was as early as 5:00am, but as a child, I was an early riser. The only channel we could get on the television back then was the ABC. If it was the weekend, Rage was on and the countdown of the top 50 songs of the week were playing. I would always find some scrap paper to write down the list, ensuring I knew all the popular songs and artists of the time.

This was a way for me to pass time before 'Jack High' started. I quickly became addicted to the skill and grace of lawn bowls. Daphne Shaw and Rob Parella were in their prime back then, along with a young Cameron Curtis and Mark McMahon. Watching bowls was my highlight of the week.

There is no doubt watching balls rolling down a green and landing near the little white ball was very strange for someone my age. I can never put a finger on what exactly drew me to the sport, but I was in love. I knew all the top players. I knew how the scoring worked. I got excited when a player would drive and understood when Parella was playing, why his opposition would block out his forehand thunderbolt. I wouldn't have missed an episode for the world.

I was always on such a high when the program finished, unable to contain my excitement. I wouldn't stop talking about it all day, even though nobody else had any interest in my rundown of the matches played. It was only the beginning of what would later become a life-long love affair with a sport that changed my world.

Martin was often riding his motorbike on the weekends and was always trying to get mum to go for a spin. Hesitant for a long time, she one day relented and finally went for a ride.

1980's fashion involved leopard skin print, miniskirts, long-sleeved loose tops, and colours like fluorescent pink and green. So, picture this; mum on the back of a motorcycle in typical 1980's clothes, flying around the caravan park with a young Maltese man, only to make an unexpected stop at a residence Martin knew too well.

There was a woman in her late forties staring in horror, as mum slid off the motorbike saddle in the most lady-like way possible. All Martin could say was, "Hi mum! This is Sally. She has two kids, and I am going to move to Melbourne with her".

They were Martin's exact words.

I wonder how embarrassing this must have been for my mum. She had finally taken the motorbike ride with Martin only to end up in a surprise meeting with his mother. Mum reckons the look on Doris' face was priceless. Her face was all scrunched, teeth were grinding, her garden gloves tossed to the sky, the shovel thrown to the flower bed, eyes wide-open and a tensed, prominently raised fist. What Doris said next is not fit to put on paper, but to say she disagreed with Martin's plan would be the understatement of the millennium. Sometimes what your mother says needs to be the brutal honesty, even if it does hurt your feelings. She was straight to the point with her opinion.

We found out a few weeks later that Doris had been asking around the caravan park for Martin. With no mobile phones around at the time, someone could easily disappear without a trace. Little did she know, Martin had packed up his things and returned to Melbourne with our little family.

It had all happened so fast. A man around the house was something we had been lacking for a while, and even though he was young at heart, he treated us kids like we were his own, right from the start. We were very lucky to be where we were in that very moment.

So, Melbourne it was.

CHAPTER 4

Lifesaver

We didn't last long in Melbourne.

South Melbourne was home for a short while, less than 200 metres from the beach. The old Arnott's biscuit factory down the road gave us an amazing scent of freshly cooked biscuits every morning. I caught up with some friends at school, but only briefly, as our new family decided to make the Central Coast of NSW our new home.

Leaving Victoria for the second time in a year had a more permanent feeling than our first trip. I was still very young and had travelled more of the east coast of Australia than most other kids my age. It would mean a new home, new school, new friends, and a totally new climate.

Our caravan in Chain Valley Bay was in a great spot. We were on the waterfront, and Doris had recently moved into a house just around the corner. We had a heated swimming pool to use, and access to some of the best fishing spots. I could catch crabs, bream, whiting, long-tons, and flathead on a handline, using only stale bread. Fishing became my new passion, and I fished every day.

We would walk as a family around the outskirts of the park, taking in all the local flora and fauna. Some of the tracks were dangerous, with soft mud near small damns and overgrown shrubs covering the walkways. My sister and I would often lag behind, enjoying the sights of the great outdoors. Our lagging would prove near fatal for me on one mild, March evening.

My feet became tangled in a patch of soft mud, and I started to sink. The more I struggled, the quicker I sank. I didn't cry out to mum or Martin until I realised I had no chance of getting out. It took Martin only a few moments to reach me after my cry, running back to give me a hand. Half of my little body had sunk below the level of the ground, and I had mere seconds before I would be completely under. Thankfully Martin had the strength to pull me free. It all happened so fast. I was too young to take in a near death experience. I didn't cry. There was no doubt though, that Martin had saved my seven-year-old life.

The bus trips to and from school were awful. My sister and I had battled to make new friends, so we would sit together and try not to draw attention to ourselves. We were picked on. We were made the victims of some shocking bullies; but we were the newbies, so had to deal with it. School was also tough. We had no-one else to play with, so had to hang out with each other during recess and lunchtime. It drew us closer together, but by the time we got home, we were sick of each other's company for the day. For the first time in my life, I felt alone. I began doing a lot of things by myself, including fishing, swimming, and bike riding. I didn't associate with anyone around the caravan park other than myself. It was the start of my social grapple and independence.

Early in Spring, Martin had come to watch me swim in the heated pool. Mum was back at the caravan taking care of my newborn brother, Beau. The weather was warm most of the year, humid, and often wet. I felt I was a competent swimmer, but I wasn't. While completing an underwater roll, I blacked out. Martin jumped in the pool fully clothed and carried me out of the water. I don't remember much about the whole thing, but again, this angel saved my life. He would jokingly tell people that he had winning TAB tickets in his pocket that were destroyed by the water. I never asked him about the accuracy of his claim, but even so, the truth should never get in the way of a good story.

By late December 1989, school was finally over for the year, and we were on summer holidays. Christmas came and went, but as usual I was spoilt with a ridiculous number of presents. I got a new bike, with no training wheels, amongst other things like clothes and toys. That Santa Clause bloke must have had me on his 'nice' list all year round.

On December 28th, shortly before 10:30am, we were at the local store picking up a few groceries. Friends and peers often say I have a photographic memory, but sometimes you witness something so extraordinary that it stays etched in the forefront of your mind forever. I saw cereal boxes flying off the shelves and breaking on the floor. I heard glass bottles clinking around the smashing sound of jars hitting the ground. The building was shaking and some of the lights were going out.

We hit the deck to avoid being hit by flying food. Martin was leaning against a huge drink fridge nearby, making sure it didn't topple onto us. It was about the only thing in the supermarket that didn't end up on the ground. The lady at the counter was screaming her head off. You could clearly hear her shrieks over the top of the destruction. What was only a few seconds, felt a hell of a lot longer. Within minutes, we heard sirens echoing outside, while many people had made their way out to the streets to check on their co-workers and neighbours. There was a total sense of confusion.

The 1989 Newcastle earthquake killed 13 people that day and 160 others were hospitalised. We didn't live in Newcastle but were less than 40km away from the epicentre at Boolaroo. What I witnessed that day, from that distance, was scary enough. I hate to imagine what those closer to Boolaroo went through.

Watching the breaking news specials that afternoon was like a horror movie. Newcastle had been torn to shreds. Buildings had cracked, crumbled, and collapsed. The massive destruction made Newcastle look like a war-torn city. The damage was catastrophic.

We never felt the small after-shock that hit the next day. As a family, we never really discussed the incident at all. It could have been the shock and severity of the situation, or seen as so tragic, that it shouldn't be spoken about. Humans are amazing like that. We have a filing system in our brain that stores some tragic memories, locked up, with no key to fit.

In the space of nine months, Martin had saved my life three times; the sinking mud, the pool accident, and now the unsteady fridge in the supermarket. I was close to turning eight, but already had distinct memories that would have a bearing on the rest of my life.

I don't swim anymore, and it took me more than two decades to begin confronting my resounding fear of water. I was petrified of open water, beaches, boats, swimming pools, and rivers. Fear can affect humans in some of the most distinctive ways.

If I was a cat, I was down to six lives. Still going strong though, I became familiar with one of the world's most compelling proverbs.

Life goes on.

CHAPTER 5

Lion

The earthquake was enough to send us packing once more.

With my grandfather organising a job for Martin on the trams, we moved back to Melbourne. We lived in a small flat in St Kilda East, close enough for my sister and I to return to our favourite primary school in Albert Park.

Mum married Martin in August 1990, and Martin became dad.

Being a young family, we needed more space than a flat, so we moved out to the west side of Melbourne and settled in the suburb of Laverton. It once again meant a new school, new friends, and a whole new start. I seemed to be starting all over again a lot for a child, which was part of the reason I became so independent.

I was enrolled at Laverton Park Primary School and assumed the Schraner surname. The school doesn't exist anymore, merging with Laverton Gardens Primary School in the mid-1990's. My new school seemed behind the times, so much so that I found the work too easy. What I was being taught in Laverton was knowledge I already had, remembering the accelerated learning schedule I went through at Albert Park, after my computer hack.

Whether academic, sporting or any other activity, I was the leader of the class. I was the captain of our school football and cricket teams and played every sport available in inter-school sport. As well as AFL and cricket, I played newcombe, tennis, bat tennis, badminton, and was a regular blue-ribbon winner on school athletics days.

Despite all this success, my fondest memory of school at the time was joining the school choir. I had a beautiful voice at that age and loved to sing. Our school choir sang at other schools, shopping centres, and even railway stations. We practiced hard after school regularly and had a solid repertoire of songs. Ms Larkin, both our choir coach and art teacher, was very proud of us. Some of us were suited to singing in the background, but not me. I was always front and centre.

In a concert held at Werribee Centenary Hall, I sang 'The Lion Sleeps Tonight' solo, in front of hundreds of people. The choir chanted the back-up gibberish, while I was out front on the microphone alone with a pair of Aboriginal clap sticks. I stood on the stage and belted the song out, having no trouble with reaching the high notes. Every word sung was done so with the utmost care and respect for the music. Under heat duress from the stage lights, and sweat pouring from my forehead, I refused to be distracted.

When the performance ended, I turned to the choir and clapped them. In the background, the crowd had jumped to their feet and erupted with applause. The ovation made all the hairs stand up on the back of my neck. My body was numb with pride. I enjoyed the moment so much that I became addicted to success. The seed was planted for a life of achievement. I didn't believe in mediocrity.

Mathew was born in July 1991 and some of the priorities in my life changed. I was now a big brother to three younger siblings. I had to be a responsible role model and give my love and care to my newest family members. I was going to be the big brother that everybody else wanted.

I had to be the best at everything I did, even if I had no natural ability. I had the determination, fight, and hunger, to be the best I could be. I strove for perfection. I had to be a winner. I had to be successful. Despite my single-digit age, I saw every situation as an opportunity to be the best. If I failed at any task, I took the time to learn what was required to be successful the next time.

My conditioning would pave the way to a positive future. My belief was that I would succeed in whatever I chose to do. I had little idea at the time about what I wanted to be when I grew up. There were too many roads to cross before jumping to such an important decision. Right then, I was spoilt for choice. My confidence was high and my stature among my friends was the highest it could be. I was the one they all looked up to.

Ego is not a dirty word.

CHAPTER 6

Haunted

We lived in two houses in Laverton during the early 1990's. One was in Sumers Street, just off the main road, and the second in Eaton Parade.

Sumers Street was a three-bedroom house on the corner, across from a court where I could kick the football and play cricket, safely away from the traffic. We were close to the main part of town, so most of my friends lived nearby and could easily walk down for kick. Not even 10, but short in stature, I could still out-run and out-kick all my friends. Football became another exciting opportunity for my teenage years, but one that would never eventuate past school level.

My sister and I shared a room in the back corner of the house. With the hardwood floors, there were often creaks and cracks in the middle of the night from the wind. The wind, however, didn't wear boots or carry chains.

Dad never told us, but we knew what lived by his fingertips every night. He had an old hockey stick from his younger days, curved end sawn off, and a three-pronged garden tool masked tightly to the end of it. You might think I'm joking, but I am deadly serious. In fact, Mum and Dad were so convinced someone or something roamed the hallway of the house, they had many nights without a wink of sleep. Some nights when we heard the steps and rattle of chains, we would also hear Dad jump up, open his door and march around the house looking for the intruder. He would generally open our bedroom door to check we were okay, holding the door in one hand while his other hand concealed the makeshift weapon behind his back. His bright, white eyes were enough to cast a ray of light at our doorway, without need for a bulb switch. Although putting on a strong face, it was clear he was petrified. Whatever roamed the vacant hallway at night was never caught, but may have attached itself to our family, as our next home in Eaton Parade went to a whole new level of supernatural.

Once the opportunity to move availed itself, we were out of Sumers Street in a flash. A couple of kilometres down the road, we settled in a smaller two-bedroom house with an enormous backyard. There was plenty of room inside our fence-line to play any sport I wanted to. Once again, my sister and I would share a bedroom, while a young Beau and Mathew were cotted up in our parent's room.

Thinking we had escaped from the haunted house in Sumers Street, we were soon starting to wonder if the invisible intruder had followed us to our new home.

The manhole in the main living room had a mind of its own. Every morning, we would get up, the manhole would be slightly ajar, and Dad would stand on the couch, closing it shut. It was maybe only open an inch or two, but enough to see it had been tampered with.

One cold June night, my sister and I both woke, staring at each other dead frightened. Just a couple of metres from our door was the entrance to the bathroom and the light was clicking on and off. Normally the bathroom light would stay on the entire night because we weren't fond of the dark.

Chantelle jumped out of her bed and into mine. She was shivering ad shaking, totally scared out of her wits. I felt no better. I was wide-eyed and struggling to breathe. We were whispering to each other about going to see what was happening. We both knew it wasn't Mum or Dad playing a joke, especially after what we had experienced in out last home.

Together we snuck out of bed and crawled to the doorway of our room. It was only three or four metres to crawl, but it definitely felt a lot further. The light was still going on and off and we could hear the constant clicking of the switch. In perfect synchronisation, we poked our heads through the bedroom doorway. The bathroom door was wide open, and we could now see the light going on and off. No-one was in the bathroom, and no-one was in the entrance. There wasn't even a shadow. What the hell was going on with the light?

We weren't going any closer. Chantelle had started sobbing silently while I began to feel my panic turn to tears. We looked at each other and I shook my head. In a split second, we had turned around and crawled back into bed together.

Suddenly a door opened, and Chantelle screamed. I pulled the doona over our heads. I couldn't watch.

Footsteps stormed down the hallway straight to the bathroom. The light stopped flicking and stayed in an 'off' position. A few moments later, the light was turned back on and through the thin doona, I could make out a figure standing in our bedroom doorway. I shrieked. Thankfully a familiar voice provided instant calm and I could lift the doona from our heads. It was Dad. The clicking must have woken him up too. I knew he was trying to hide it behind his back, but the makeshift hockey-spear had made its way across from Sumers Street. There was no accusation. He knew it wasn't us playing with the light. He simply asked if we were okay and then told us to try and go back to sleep. You could see the alarming alertness in his eyes. This is the sort of stuff that would bring grown men to their knees, but not Dad. His bravery existed to care for the well-being of his family.

The sun came up and Chantelle and I began getting ready for school. Once again, the manhole was slightly ajar. We didn't speak a word about the night in hope that it was just a terrible nightmare.

While making breakfast, we could hear Mum and Dad having a conversation in their bedroom. Beau and Mathew were awake, both crying in their cots. It was difficult to make out what they were saying to each other.

Dad opened their bedroom door and marched his way to the shed, clearly a man on a mission. Minutes later he re-appeared with a silicon glue gun, a clamp, a hammer, and some long nails. He moved the couch under the manhole and started work. He glued the manhole down with silicon and hammered in no less than a dozen nails. That thing was stuck so tight, it had no chance of being opened without some serious strength. He went about his business without saying a word.

On returning from school that afternoon, we were told by Mum and Dad that they were looking for a new house away from Laverton. With Dad working on the trains and trams and making good money, we finally had enough saved to escape rentals and put a deposit on a house. They both spoke about Melton and the opportunities that existed there for young families. With decent properties available at affordable prices, multiple schools, and more facilities than Laverton, Melton seemed a feasible option for us.

Weeks went by and then months. The manhole had not moved. The silicon and nails had closed it tight. The bathroom light never flicked, and no strange events occurred in the house. Life went on in normal fashion.

In November of 1993, Mum and Dad gave us the exciting news that we had been approved for a mortgage on a house in Melton. We had a month to pack things up and make our way to an exciting new home.

School wound up late in November for both my sister and me. With the two of us top of our classes, missing the last three or four weeks of school for the year wasn't going to hurt us.

Our final night in Laverton will live forever in my memory, and not for the right reasons. The moving truck was due in early at 7:00am so we had all set alarms for six.

At exactly five minutes to six, right before our alarms started buzzing, the whole house was woken to a massive crash and bang coming from the living room. My sister and I both jumped up, running down the hall to see what had woken us so suddenly. Standing at the living room door was Mum and Dad, about to open the door. After we all stared each other down and took a couple of deep breaths, Dad opened the door.

Instantaneously, four jaws dropped.

There was a small puff of dust in the air and a strong smell of mothballs and dirt. The manhole sat in the centre of the floor unhinged, unstuck, and completely detached from its home in the roof. And that's right where we left it - on the floor!

That was enough for us to start throwing boxes of belongings onto the front lawn, even before the moving truck had arrived. We didn't want to spend one-minute longer in that house than we had too.

By 8:00am we were fully loaded and in the car on the way to Melton. Hopefully the demons we encountered in Laverton wouldn't follow us to our new home. What we had just experienced was not for the faint-hearted. A living nightmare of a supernatural source that had a bone to pick with someone or something, taking its bad temper out on our young family. Prayers and religion wouldn't have been enough to clear the air in that house. It would have needed a full property-exorcism. I didn't even wave goodbye as we left.

Adios to the ghost!

CHAPTER 7

Melton

Melton provided the freedom a young family needed in the early 1990's. Housing was affordable; all the basic facilities were there, and schooling was fit for all levels of education. I was enrolled at Kurunjang Secondary College in year seven, which was to our information, the best public school in Melton.

I did have the opportunity of travelling to Galvin Park Secondary in Werribee, where I had won a scholarship just a few months earlier, but the travel would be a massive burden.

The first day of high school was supposed to be the scariest day of my life. I was starting at a new school, in a new suburb, with people I didn't know.

My first day will only be remembered for one thing – I was the only one in the entire school to turn up! With a school bag full of every book I had, I arrived at school with no idea of what subjects

I would face on day one. My bag weighed as much as I did, but I was there and ready to learn.

After walking around for a few minutes and not seeing a soul, I decided to make my way to the school office. A friendly female teacher with a huge smirk on her face was kind enough to tell me that the primary school was starting that day, but the high school was not starting until tomorrow. How embarrassing!

I rang home but no-one was there. I suppose Dad had gone to work and Mum and Pop were still at the primary school dropping my sister off for her first day of grade five. I had an idea. I would stand back outside the front of the high school and wave down the green Ford station wagon as it made its way back toward home. If I missed it, then all I had to do was go back to the office, redial home and hope to God someone was there.

To my luck, Pop's car cruised past the front of Kurunjang Secondary and I flagged it down. I was literally all dressed up with no place to go, except home to relax for one more day. I felt like a moron. I can understand turning up to school a day late, but to be there a day early is just ridiculous.

At 6:30am the next morning, my alarm went off and this time I was getting ready for my 'real' first day. It was a Thursday morning and only two days separated me from my first weekend of homework.

My first day involved Art, Humanities, Graphics and Maths. I hated art. I hated everything about art. I couldn't draw and I had no interest in painting, clay, or any other creation. I was a teenager who liked words and numbers. To make matters worse, my art teacher was a full-grown bitch. All she cared about was sipping on her coffee and yelling "Shut Up!" at the top of her voice. I never had a teacher like this before. I was always a teacher's pet. A new start in a new school meant I had to earn my brownie points all over again. I wasn't going to bother doing that with art. I had no interest in it other than manipulating my way to an 'A' somehow, but not by befriending this teacher.

By the weekend I had racked up about 3,000 hours of homework. I always did my homework, came to class prepared and never fell behind in any subject. I was dedicated to my schoolwork and took no short-cuts on any of the tasks. This was my way of showing teachers and students that I was there to learn and not to muck around.

I didn't make any friends in the first few weeks, but after a while I noticed the kids who were as isolated as me in the classroom and school yard. It was time to introduce myself to someone who needed a friend too.

Only very few know this, but I made a friendship at school that lasted for many years. This red-headed, tall sports star was neglected just like I was by our peers. He too was the oldest child in his family and obviously, the first of his siblings to start high school. Although not a nerd like me, he certainly tried his best with every subject. The fact that he was sporty, friendly, and gave it his all in everything he did, meant we would form a great friendship. Robert Doody and I became the best of friends in late February of 1994.

My mid-year report at school was a shambles in my eyes. Rather than focusing on the 22 A's I had got, I couldn't turn away from the two B's and a D. I was always a straight A student, so marks below that created concern among my parents. The two B's were in Art, and the D was in Textiles. That's right, bloody Textiles! Quite simply, I didn't have a great relationship with cross-stitch, fabric, and sewing machines. I even made the teacher cry when I cut a whole roll of fabric the wrong way and wasted metres of material.

The highlight of my first year of high school was making the Junior (Year 7 & 8) football team. I was the shortest in the team and probably the skinniest.

After spending three quarters and 20 minutes on the bench, my coach finally let me on the ground. When the score is 0 to 255, you don't exactly run onto the ground feeling as though you can make a difference.

It belted rain all day, was about seven degrees, and we had the pleasure of kicking into a howling gale in the final quarter. After yet another goal was scored against us, the ball came back to the centre circle. Our ruck was flattened and scored a free kick.

He was lucky to kick 20 metres into the wind, but in a moment of fortune, it landed on the chest of Doody. He turned and ran. He bashed the ball well inside the 50-metre arc and it tumbled to about 15 metres from goal. As the ball hadn't been down there all game, there was not one player in site. It was a foot race between me and their little rover. I knew I was quick and with a tank full of gas, I wasn't about to lose this run at the ball.

We sprinted nothing short of 30 metres side by side. I shut my eyes as I slid through the mud to kick the ball off the ground at goal. Mud covered me from head to toe. As I opened my eyes, I was past the goal-line, only a metre or so short of the fence. As I wiped the mud from my eyes, I turned around to see the goal umpire waving a single white flag above his head. It wasn't a goal, but the behind had got us on the scoreboard.

In that moment, the siren went, and all our team ran towards me. They lifted me up chanting and carried me off the ground, shorts still half-way up my back and muddy cheeks hanging out the reverse-side of my shorts. I had become a cult hero. I was the little fella who got us off the dreaded zero and saved us from absolute embarrassment. I would only learn in days to come that it was the first time our junior team had scored in years. Melton Secondary had slaughtered us year after year without letting us score.

I was awarded best player on the ground for our team for my one disposal and one point. I made many new friends after that day. In stature, I looked up to them, but in reality, I was a totem pole. All the boys in the team would look up to me from that day forward.

We may have lost by 260 points on that freezing June day in 1994, but memories of what it did for me moving forward, will always stay with me. It was quite simply the greatest ever point scored by a Kurunjang Secondary junior footballer.

Well that's my story and I'm sticking to it.

CHAPTER 8

Dust

It was late November 1994, about four weeks before the school year ended when Mum sprung a surprise on me.

Mum came home on a Thursday night with a Royal Victorian Bowls Association (RVBA) Open Day flyer to Mount Cottrell Bowling Club, a single-greened synthetic club in Rockbank famous for its extraordinary wind speeds. Remembering my days in the caravan with lawn bowls on the television, Mum offered to take me to the bowling club that Sunday to give the game a try.

It was the first Sunday in December and despite hardly sleeping the night before, I was chomping at the bits to play my first lawn bowl. I jumped in the car with Mum late morning, and we headed to the bowling club. We got onto the Western Freeway and turned right down Mount Cottrell Road; according to the map, the club was down there.

At 30 kilometres an hour, we drove down the bumpiest, driest, pothole filled, rough dirt road you have ever seen in your life. Quite simply, the road was dangerous and the dust flying over the car was disgraceful. The vibrations from the road were horrific. We drove about ten minutes before I told Mum to turn around and forget it. There was no way a bowling club could be this isolated. We had no idea where the club was and nothing more than a street directory to guide us.

To my delight, Mum persevered and a couple of minutes later we came to a property on our left-hand-side, gated, with a tiny little sign showing 'Mount Cottrell Bowls Club'. Unbelievably, we had arrived.

The single synthetic green was about 50 metres from the clubhouse, fenced around and adjacent to the unsurfaced carpark. The green had about a dozen people on it, playing bowls, trying bowls and others giving instructions. A man named "George" was first to approach us and introduce himself. He began explaining the basics of the game to my mother; the bias of the bowl, the weight of the bowl and how to place the bowl in your hand. He demonstrated how to aim the bowl, step, and release, saying right from the start that you had to reach the jack and not be short of it.

Mum didn't have the heart to tell him, so I rudely interrupted and told him that I was the one here to try bowls. George was pleasantly surprised but looking at scrawny little 12-year-old kid probably didn't attract his interest as much as my 31-year-old mother. George was a very friendly man, even to me. He took me on the bowling green, showed me how to place the mat, roll the jack and then the basics of grass-line and how the bias worked. All I wanted to do was bowl, not listen to a lecture.

I checked one final time with him about which side of the bowl had the bias and then took the time to play my first ever lawn bowl. I will never forget holding the size four heavyweight classic deluxe bowl, with a motif of an old-fashioned Rolls Royce motor vehicle. It was the first lawn bowl I ever held, so I took the time to appreciate it.

My first bowl was heavy and narrow. My second bowl touched the jack. My third bowl was a wrong bias and my fourth and final bowl landed right next to the jack. A small crowd of club members and visitors gathered around as I played another five ends or so by myself. They were smiling, clapping, and even cheered loudly whenever I got one close to the jack. There was no doubt that 12-year-olds playing bowls in the mid 1990's was very rare, especially one who had some idea of the game itself. In fairness, I looked much younger than my age. Some may have thought I was only eight or nine years old.

George invited Mum and I into the clubhouse where we had sausage sandwiches for lunch. Mum got me a soft drink at the bar, and we sat with George at an empty trestle table. Membership of the club was $50 for a season. I totally freaked out. $50 was a massive amount of money and I knew Mum didn't have that kind of money to spend on a lawn bowls membership. Membership aside, I would also need a set of bowls, whites to bowl in, bowls cloth, chalk, bowling shoes, and a bowls bag. Even today, bowls remains one of the most expensive sports to get started and it was no different back then. Although disappointed at the time, I knew with that kind of financial outlay, bowls was a sport that I couldn't afford to play.

The next day, a Monday, I went to the Newsagency after school to buy some coloured paper for my science project. In the newsagency was George, the same man who taught me how to play bowls the day before.

George Arnold owned the Melton Newsagency.

Little to my knowledge, Mount Cottrell was struggling for membership and to find enough players for their upcoming Saturday pennant match. I told him that I enjoyed the experience and would love to play in a game, but the financial commitment of starting up was an issue for our young family. He gave me the coloured paper I needed with no charge and insisted I leave the financial issues with him. He was a pennant selector and unless they could get a player for Saturday, their lowest grade may have to forfeit.

That Thursday, I got home from school and George was sitting at the dining room table with Mum and Pop having a coffee. I don't know how long he had been there, but he was about to give me the greatest gift I had ever received. He handed me a carry bag with my very own set of lawn bowls. They were a size four heavyweight set of Henselite classics, with a motif of a gold star encased in a shell. Inside the bag was also a bowls measure, chalk, Grippo, a bowls cloth, a white cap, and a small white polo shirt. I basically had all the equipment I needed to start playing bowls. That, and George had also paid my membership at Mount Cottrell. Wow!

That Friday after school, Mum drove me to the op-shop in Melton South, on the lookout for some white cricket pants or trousers. We found some in my size for $3.00. I didn't have bowling shoes yet, but because I was selected to play away on the Melton artificial, I would be able to wear some flat-soled runners.

I was in my whites and black runners, ready to go very early on Saturday morning. Dad took me out in the front yard where he took photos of me holding the bowl and pretending to roll it on the lawn. Nan also got in the photos with me, proud of her Grandson. Sadly, those photographs have been misplaced these days, but the memories remain.

Noon arrived and so did George to pick me up. It was a very warm day in Melton on 10th December 1994, reaching about 30 degrees. We were playing in a division four match against Melton, which was the lowest grade in the Central Highlands pennant competition. I was playing lead against a guy named Lenny Kean, a guy still well-known for his competitive game style. I befriended him pretty quickly because he was clever enough to bring two frozen bottles of cordial. I had no money for drinks, so it was either the water bubbler or the frozen drink Lenny had offered me.

I don't remember the score from the match. I do, however, remember two key things; one, I played terrible and hardly got any bowls near the jack, and two, we were absolutely belted on the two rinks and didn't score any team points. The score didn't matter that much. I had played my first game of pennant lawn bowls and me being there, gave the other seven players a match, instead of forfeiting.

When George dropped me home that evening, he told me to try and get down to the club for Wednesday night twilight bowls as much as I could. That way I could learn from the more experienced bowlers and hopefully pick the game up a bit quicker. I certainly needed a lot more training and social bowls before I could consider playing pennant for the club again. Thankfully, they had enough for the following Saturday, and I could have the final match off before the Christmas break.

I made twilight bowls that Wednesday and met two very friendly members, Rod and Lorraine Quinn. They offered to pick me up and drop me off anytime I wanted to play Twilight Bowls, an open, mixed competition of about 12 or so members.

I was always playing lead, as I should have been, learning to roll the jack and draw as close as possible. I met some great people such as, Clive and Adele Brown, Nancy and Ernie Williams, Hughie Hoare, Roy and Shirley Doyle, and many others. For just $3.00, we got a game of bowls, a sausage sizzle, and the chance to win a bowls cloth or club whiskey glass. I always wanted to win, but being so new, I was often the one who cost our team the chance of taking home the prize.

Twilight bowls ran all through the Christmas break and I never missed a week. I played right up until the end of the pennant season. Even starting year eight at high school was no barrier. I always made the time to find a way to the bowls club and practice. I had to get better at the game if I wanted to play pennant the next season.

My best mate at school, Robert, was getting annoyed that I had no time to catch up on the weekends or after school. I was either wrapped up in homework or down at the bowling club having a roll. I told him I was playing lawn bowls and showed him the bowls cloth and glass I had won at twilight bowls.

In the end, curiosity got the better of him and he joined me for a game of twilight bowls. There was no doubt that he had more natural ability than I did. He was a star in whatever sport he played. They put him in at lead and he was able to draw constantly close to the jack in his very first game. This friendly rivalry between us could only make us become better bowlers moving forward.

Our friendship was growing, and we wanted to play bowls together. For this reason, we entered the 1995 winter pennant competition at the club. We put Robert down as lead, me as second, and left the third and skip spot vacant for anyone to take. We needed two other players to make a team, but unfortunately every time we checked the entry sheet on the board, those two spots continued to remain blank. It appeared that May would arrive before we had a team, and we would miss out on playing.

Eventually two names filled those spots. A man named Les Delaney from Flemington-Kensington Bowls Club, as well as Ernie Williams from our club, put their names down to play with us. It was so exciting to have a team. We were called 'Composite' as we had members from two different clubs. The Winter couldn't arrive quick enough for Robert and I. We were so excited to begin a competition playing together.

It was time to make a mark on the sport.

CHAPTER 9

Nev

The winter pennant season for our Composite team was more of a number-filling effort than a chance at a premiership. Both Robert and I were first year players and after Ernie gave up on us, we struggled to find a regular third. Our saviour every Sunday was the super-skip himself, Les Delaney. Les was a division one or two bowler from Flemington-Kensington who put his hand up week in and week out to play with us young kids. To us, he was the God of bowls. He had more talent than our entire bowling club put together.

Daylesford entered a winter pennant team the same season. They had this young kid leading for them and he couldn't have been any older than about 10 or 11. It was obvious he had some ability, and being the only other player around our age, we soon befriended him.

When the matches were done, Robert and I would do the same as we always did. We would head inside, drink free cups of tea, have our sausage sizzle, and get straight back on the green for our driving extravaganza. Most of the other players would stay inside and drink pots of beer, while the non-drinkers generally left after the daily presentations.

To make our after-game fun more interesting, we asked the young fella from Daylesford to join us on the green. I will never know if he did it out of boredom or pity, but he jumped out of his seat and headed out to the green with us.

It is funny how you cross paths with certain people at different times in your life. I mean, knowing today compared to what I knew then, I would never have picked the fate and longevity of what has become a lifelong friendship.

The young Daylesford kid called himself 'Nev'. I had no idea what his last name was at the time, or even if 'Nev' was his actual name, but the driving contest outside had hit a whole new level. Of course, playing on the front end of rinks, we never got the chance to play attacking shots during a match. This was our release of fun, albeit to fill the time in until our lift was ready to take us home.

Before Nev left for home, we grabbed his phone number and had a plan to have a game together someday soon. This was almost 29 years ago and no doubt, the Lee Schraner and Neville Rodda pairs partnership on a bowling green has come a very long way since our first meeting at Mount Cottrell in 1995. I knew there was something about this kid that seemed different from a lot of others. He had a clear desire to achieve on the bowling green, not to just rock up and throw lead bowls down.

From day one on the green, I always told myself that I was going to play for Australia. Nev seemed to have similar goals and it wasn't long before he had the legendary Don Sherman Senior onboard, coaching him to Victorian Under 18 titles.

Our bowling partnership earnt us the 2011 Australian Open Pairs Gold Medal, a 2010 NSW Open Pairs Silver Medal, and many other good results in tournaments across the country. In March 2011, we were the Number one and two Pairs players in Australia according to the ranking system at the time. We would eventually attempt start-up businesses together that unfortunately fell-through, with Nev moving to Wellington, New Zealand, running a successful website business with his partner Felicity. We keep regular contact today via facebook, always having a joke and reminiscing about days gone by. What we achieved together would set the foundation for a lifelong bond.

When the winter pennant finished in August, we were only weeks away from the summer pennant practice matches. School was the main priority, but if I kept my grades at the highest level, Mum and Dad had no reason to stop me from playing bowls. The key was to ensure a balance between the two, where I could achieve in sport and studies at the same time.

After the practice matches, both Robert and I were selected in the bottom side as leads. Our first pennant match together would be at Bacchus March, on grass, which we had never played on, let alone even seen.

I was leading for Ray Blackeby, and our rink was getting slaughtered. Robert was leading for Eddie Knight, and they were a mile in front. Down 7-33, our rink piled on 15-0 over the last five ends to reduce our margin to negative 11. Eddie's team won by 17, which meant we had won overall by six shots. Our first game on grass and our first ever pennant win. We couldn't help but smile like Chesire cats. After barely getting a win all winter, we had started the summer season with a flyer.

By the Christmas break, both Robert and I found ourselves promoted to lead in the division two team, our club's top side. Our first year of bowls together and we would make it with the best bowlers in our club. Maybe we were going to make it big in the game.

But we were never going to make it big at little old Mount Cottrell.

CHAPTER 10

Reality

In early 1996, after starting year nine at school and turning 14, I knew deep down that my life would never be the same again. I had lost my free-living sense and innocence as a teenager, convinced that I had become an outcast with serious issues. What started as a sense of jealousy, interest, and strange urges, was about to become an obsession.

The day you wake up and realise you are different from everyone else can be very scary for a young teenager. Despite how good your family, friends, sport, and studies are, the sense of loneliness in your personal life can drive you to independence and isolation.

It can tear you to pieces.

It can grab your every thought.

It is an overwhelming and unwelcome want that becomes part of you.

I knew 14-years-old that I was gay, and it was affecting me in a way that only a gay person could ever understand. My major concern at that age was that I was not willing to accept it. I was a school sports star, an intelligent young man, masculine and manly in the way I spoke and acted. I tried to write the feelings off as a 'phase' or a 'part' of growing up, but I couldn't escape the hormones, wants, and needs.

I reacted in a way that only someone in denial would. There was a girl at school named Melissa and she was a good friend of mine. I had to put myself to the ultimate test, so I asked her out to the movies. I never had a girlfriend before, but I was determined to see if my urges were misplaced or unjustified. I really liked Melissa as a friend but had never been attracted to her in any way. Whether I had an intimate connection or not, I just needed to know where I stood. I had to be certain I could be comfortable in a relationship with a woman.

To my thrill, Melissa accepted my proposition saying that she had a massive crush on me.

We went to the movies once or twice, kissed a few times, and I even went over to her house. Her mum and my mum were good friends, so they both would have been happy to see us together. The main concern for me was that all this intimacy and interaction gave me no positive feelings whatsoever. I felt uncomfortable, disinterested, and like I was forcing myself to be someone that I wasn't. My urges and hormones were flowing, but not for Melissa or any other female for that matter.

I went into my shell as a human through year nine. I focused even more on my studies and bowls than ever before. I was doing everything I could to keep myself distracted from thinking about anything sexual. But it wouldn't go away. It was never going away.

My school report scored 48 A's out of a possible 48 in 1996.

Without needing to draw a picture for everyone to see, I was a teenager that needed relief from my urges and feelings. All I could think about in those moments were things I didn't want to think about. I was often grossing myself out to the point of throwing up. Being in denial about who you are is a great way to make yourself sick. It not only affects you physically, but mentally it is extremely dangerous.

I was angry that I had been dealt this card. I was upset that it had happened to me. The thing I was most cut about was that I didn't have a choice in the matter. I would have given a leg or an arm at the time to be straight. I even considered physical harm to take away from the mental torture.

I felt abnormal. I wasn't born as a human being to function this way. It was like I was the only gay person in the world. Even in the

1990's homosexuality was taboo. If you were gay, you didn't tell anyone. You hid it from family and friends in fear.

I had no idea what to do. I thought about getting some professional help or advice but was so embarrassed that I couldn't tell a soul. More to the point, I wouldn't dare tell a soul. I was prepared at that point in time to live in denial and pretend to be normal like everybody else.

Days would pass and my urges would only get stronger. I would pray, cry, whimper, to any spirit that would listen. I couldn't live like this. I wouldn't wish it on my worst enemy. It broke me as a human.

I wouldn't say that I was ever suicidal because I was gay, but those thoughts did cross my mind on a regular basis. The millennium was approaching, and I prayed that when it came, the world would end, and I could take my secret to the grave. I wanted the feelings to go away, but never wanted to kill myself. My life in essence, was lost.

It took many months, but I finally gave in to my thoughts. It was not like I accepted the matter, but I was too tired and weak to fight it any longer. Being as weak as I was inside, I knew that if I didn't give in to 'the devil' that my life would never amount to anything.

My theory was simple. Keep my private life to myself and never talk to anyone about it. Despite how much it built up inside, I would maintain the secret until the time was right. I needed to grow up and be more educated on the issue before I came to any short-term, stupid conclusions. This was the most sensible decision I ever made as a teenager. For my age, it was a very mature approach.

No one at school ever caught my eye for being attractive. I was more interested in AFL footballers and Australian cricketers. I could watch footy and cricket and please two of my cravings at the same time – sport and good-looking men.

I honestly believe that bottling this issue was the cause of my first nervous breakdown.

I should have been an Oscar-winning actor. From age 14 to 22, I put on an eight-year charade worthy of a golden statuette. I was confident, arrogant, dedicated, and excited with sport. I knew I was intelligent and made a mockery of schoolwork. It was too easy.

By placing my focus on the things I loved, I honestly believed the issue would sort itself out over time. Right now, all I had to keep doing was play lawn bowls, play my keyboard, write stories, watch television, and star in my studies. My private life would stay exactly that.

Sexuality is much more accepted today than it was back then. I can only imagine what it would have been like in earlier decades, and how gay people dealt with it back then. Australia even approved same-sex marriage in December 2017, highlighting a Nation that supported their inhabitants, no matter their sexuality.

One of the biggest causes of suicide in Australia is poor mental health. I have no doubt that many young Australian's who take their own life, have their mental state affected severely by their sexuality. There is not a thing that can make you smile. The whole world is on top of you. Life as you know it is over. Trust me, I have been there.

I can only advise confused teenagers that eventually, things do get better. You learn more about the statistics and commonality, understanding that you are not alone. There are many people in your life who care about you and your battles. Don't fight it alone. You will accept who you are by dismissing sexuality and labels as non-important. It might not happen straight away, but it will happen.

Time really does heal all wounds.

You are unique, you are you.

You only get one life so you may as well make the most of it. After all, it's a lot better than the alternative.

It's what's inside that counts.

CHAPTER 11

Mentor

Ironically, I met another friend named Neville just before the winter pennant started in 1996. He became a huge influence on my life in sport through that period.

Neville Thorne was a relatively new bowler who had come across to Mount Cottrell from Pascoe Vale. He was looking for a game that winter and offered to play with Robert, Les, and I as the newly labelled Mount Cottrell Brown. Even after the disaster year as 'Composite', we had roped poor Les in again for another season.

Neville was a front-end player like us two kids. We all sat down and agreed that Robert would lead, Neville would play second, and I would play third. Our only option for a skipper of course, was Les.

We all hit it off quickly and started to win a few games. This must have been a huge relief to Les who had constant headaches of negative heads just twelve months before. Fair to say though that

Robert and I had improved somewhat and the excitement of a new player in the team as handy as Neville, only made us gain belief that we could win.

Besides the interaction with Neville on the green, I also formed a very close friendship that continued for many years to come. Neville was a great sportsman in his own right. He had achieved good results in cricket as a bowler, and football as a ruckman. He was also a seriously good coach in both formats. He coached the famous Madden brothers in their junior football careers and had a lot of great advice and information for me as a junior lawn bowler.

He became my mentor.

I would call Neville at least once a week on the home phone and we would often talk for well over an hour. I would talk about issues in my life and with my bowls and he would provide me with sound advice and coaching, all to help me in my decision making. He became a huge asset in my life.

After a successful winter campaign, we made the final four but were knocked out by the all-conquering Gisborne Red side. The performance, however, was a sign of better things to come. We lost no fans going from wooden spooners to finals players in just one year.

Les didn't play pennant for Mount Cottrell, but our own pennant selectors cleverly put Robert, Neville, and me as the front three players in one rink. Instead of Les, we had one of our club's best skips, John Banks, take the helm. 'Banksy' was one of the toughest skips at the club. He made us work for every shot and certainly voiced his opinion for all to hear when we made a mistake. He was more critical than positive, so we all learnt to grow thicker skin from the very beginning.

Robert only lasted a couple of games before he pulled the pin on our rink. He had confided in our most placid skip, John McKenzie, and requested to be moved away from Banksy. Neville was pushed back to lead and the current club champion Don McDonald, came into our rink as a second. His skill and experience would be a great settling influence on Neville and I. He was able to calm us both down when Banksy fired us up.

I can't say I had much of an idea at the time, but I know now that Don and Neville became good friends. They must have visited the selectors together, requesting a move away from cranky Banksy. They were successful. Reggie Burns took over our rink as skip, starting a run of eleven straight rink wins for us. Even though we made the finals, we were knocked out by Trentham at Sunbury and another flag had gone begging for our division two club. Our rink had performed well beyond expectations, especially with me playing third so young, and so early in my bowls career. Strangely enough, it was Banksy who got flogged in the finals and played a big part in seeing us knocked out.

I made the club singles final but fell just four shots short against our club's best player Geoff Stewart. It was the first of just two losses in club singles finals that I would experience in my lifetime, but being just 15 years of age, it was more of an achievement than a failure.

Neville and I would continue to discuss things closely over the phone. I needed to consider making a move to a stronger club so that my game would continue to develop. I had made friends with David George and his sons from Footscray Park during the winter, helping me decide to move.

I would start, and then continue to play indoor biased bowls for Mount Cottrell, but for the next season of pennant, I was going to sign with Footscray Park and play my first year of metropolitan bowls. Obviously carless and unlicensed, I would rely on Melton residents who played there to transport me the 30-minute journey to and from the club.

I had to feed my ego.

CHAPTER 12

Parkers

Footscray Park gave me the opportunity of a lifetime.

There were some amazing players at my new club. Brett Dodd was an up-and-coming youngster, Robbie Campbell had just won the State Champion of Champions Singles title the year before with Footscray RSL, Glen Maxwell was a talent, and Hank Witkowski was as solid on the draw as anyone I had ever seen. Considering our top side was only Metropolitan division two, we were expected to make the leap into division one for the season to follow.

The practice matches were nothing short of a disaster for me. After two years on fast synthetic greens, the heavy grass green practice matches made it very difficult for me to find any rhythm. I was inconsistent, generally short of the jack, and not doing the job expected of me as a lead. There was no way I could possibly start in the top side.

I started the season leading in our second side which was division five. My skip was Darryl Carter, and we were drawn to play round one at Newport. Darryl was not only a great player, but a terrific skipper and gentleman. He gave me all the encouragement I needed to improve my game and find some form. He had become my new 'Les Delaney'.

By round five, I got a promotion into the top side who had struggled at the start of the season. I was leading for Pat Considine. Our third was Les Taylor and our second was Gary Dawson. On paper, we seemed like a strong side, but unfortunately the rink had underperformed, and the pressure was on me to help change that.

This was the beginning of the good times at Footscray Park. The green speeds started to increase, and my leading was improving by the week. I felt that now I had earnt a place in the top side through good bowling and would hopefully stay there for the rest of the season.

In late November, just three games into my stint in division two, I got myself a job on Saturday mornings at the local 'discount' shop in Melton, to earn some much-needed pocket money.

That first shift I worked, I got stuck back well after my 11:00am finish time and missed my lift to pennant. I had to get my grandfather to rush me down to Maribyrnong Park. I was ten minutes late to the game and missed the roll-up ends. Overall, we were soundly beaten on a slow deck and heads were about to roll.

Robbie and the selectors had no sympathy for me when the axe came out. I was dropped into division five for disciplinary reasons and told to quit my Saturday morning work if I ever wanted to play in the top side again. This infuriated me. I had no money, so the job was going to give me the few dollars I needed for bowls. I was stuck between a rock and a hard place.

That next game, I played third in division five, with a young Ryan 'Noodle' Wickson leading in our rink. This was like playing third at Mount Cottrell. The level was about the same and besides a few Central Highland stars, the level reminded me of the season before. I felt as though I was treading water and not developing as I had hoped. I considered going back to Mount Cottrell so I could keep my job, but in the end as usual, bowls took priority.

I quit my job and relayed that information to Robbie and the selectors. Division two had bounced back with a strong win at home, so I was left in division five. Luckily for me the club singles championship had arrived, and I was determined to show what I had to offer.

And I did.

After getting through the first couple of rounds, I lined up a quarter final with the champion from the previous year, Lindsay Murphy. All I could think about that week was winning the game. I can honestly say that my memory of the pennant game that Saturday remains a blur. I was distracted and had my mind focused on only one thing, beating Lindsay on Sunday.

I won the quarter final and went on to beat Hank Witkowski that afternoon in the semi-final. With just one Sunday left before Christmas, I had set up a club singles final with 1996/97 State Champion of Champions, Robbie Campbell. This was my opportunity to prove a point.

The final had it all. There was solid draw bowling, accurate hitting, and the 80 strong crowd of onlookers were enjoying the display. I will never forget that match.

After a titanic tussle, Robbie was on the verge of victory at 24-19. Two tight draw bowl saves and two big hits on the drive got me to 22-24, but my valiant attempts to save the game the following end would fail. I missed out by just three shots in the final, the last club singles final I ever lost in my career. The praise from all watching, as well as Robbie himself, was pleasing. The club singles runner-up paved my way for a spot back in division two for the first game after Christmas.

Christmas came and went, and I turned 'sweet 16' on the first game back. We racked up a few wins together as a side, but by round 18, it appeared we had no chance of top spot, and a ticket to the finals. We lay four points behind Werribee in second and 7 points behind Yarraville/Seddon in first. All we could do was try and get the maximum 14 points and hope for a miracle. Considering

Werribee and Yarraville/Seddon were playing each other in the last round, the winner of that match was most likely the winner of the section.

Call it fate, but we won our match 14-0 by about 60 shots, while down the road Yarraville/Seddon and Werribee played a 7-7 draw. We finished on top by shot differential and amazingly earnt a finals place and a promotion into division one for next season. Unbelievable!

In the Metropolitan quarter finals of division two, we comfortably beat Buckley Park at Flemington/Kensington. The next week we got past Murrumbeena Park at Glenferrie Hill and set up a grand final with Boronia at Burwood. We had adopted the club song 'Zippity-Doo-Dah' and it was sung regularly throughout the club during our finals campaign.

Unfortunately for us, it rained the night before the grand final and the slow green proved to be our nemesis. Boronia were too good, especially on our rink. We got flogged and Pat ended up calling our third Charlie down to call the head after half-time. Other rinks went well, and we probably should have won the match at 10 shots up overall with 10 ends to go. Two drops of five shots across the rinks and a string of unlucky results, and we had to be content with runners-up.

Despite our loss, the Chernobyl Victims mini-bus that we hired as a team, would make the trek back to Footscray with open drink coolers and loud renditions of 'Zippity-Doo-Dah'. So, picture this – a mini-bus full of drunken and disappointed bowlers bellowing out in song down Swan Street Richmond, with 'Chernobyl Nuclear Disaster Victims' painted across the side of the vehicle. The attention was real. We had cars pullover and trams stop in their tracks, with people laughing their heads off. It turned the mood jovial and the disappointment of the day on the green was lost in those moments. It was time to celebrate a great season and forget about our disaster finish on the green.

My oh my, what a wonderful day!

CHAPTER 13

Gold

That off-season I played indoor biased bowls pennant for Mount Cottrell. Pop and I use to go down every Friday night for a game of social bowls, often selected to play together. I'm sure he enjoyed the bowls, but I know deep down, the only reason he went was to take me there and spend some time with his favourite grandchild.

I made the decision to enter the Junior State Singles played at West Sunshine Community Centre. Sunshine wasn't far down the road from Melton, so the travel was no issue. I even talked Robert into entering as well, so we could both have a shot at the title.

On the morning of the championship, Pop picked me up from home bright and early. My first-round game was at 8:30am and it was freezing cold. There were about 15 or 16 entries in the event which meant I needed to win four games to get the gold. I saw this as a chance to get my first State level title and wanted to make the most of the opportunity. I was very confident with indoor bowls and had developed a real knack for the game.

Robert was knocked out in the first round by Shaun Membery from Warrnambool who seemed to be a young star of indoor bowls. I won my first two rounds comfortably, reaching 30 shots in each match of 16 ends. I heard a few rumours around the mats that Victoria may have found a new junior player for Nationals – they were talking about me. Looking at past results, the Victorian juniors had been smashed left, right and centre, at the last few Nationals.

I played Shaun in the semi-final and despite a tight first half of the match, I broke away to win 18-10. Nervous in the final, I fell over the line against Scott Rutherford 17-12. It was my first State title of any kind, so I was obviously exhilarated.

In the weeks following, I was invited to attend the State Junior trials to decide the two Victorians to go to the Nationals in August. Six players were invited back, and we played each other in a round robin format. I won all five games and finished on top of the pool. Robert finished second and Shaun Membery finished third. The selectors announced the team later that day and unfortunately Robert missed out. It would be Shaun and myself heading to Noosa in August to represent the 'Big V'.

Thanks to some sponsorship efforts from Sylvia Veal and the Mount Cottrell Bowls Club, my 'pay your own way trip' was covered without any expense to me. It was the first time I ever flew on a plane, and I did not enjoy the experience at all. My dislike of flying continues today.

I played Noel Wraight from New South Wales in the first match, which I won 31-9. In my second pool game, I was put against the previous year winner Brett Davis from South Australia. I had watched his first game and noticed he was unbeatable on longer ends. I knew the only way I could compete was to play the minimum length of just over 20 feet. I had to roll that length and nail my first bowl. It was a quality game for kids, but my first bowl proved the difference in a 24-10 win. It was a great start to my national campaign, even earning me the 'Vic Pick' award for Victoria's player of the day.

The Queensland humidity started to take its toll and I scraped through my third-round game 22-20 over Lennon Scott from Tasmania, now a club-mate of mine at Raymond Terrace. Only Tony Williams from Queensland stood in the way of my quest to make the final, and I had to play him the following morning.

Friday came and nerves certainly got the better of me. Tony beat me 24-22, but the result seemed closer than it really was after I grabbed a maximum four shots on the final end of the game. He became the only undefeated player in our pool. With my four games done and a bye awaiting me, my chances of making the final had slipped through my fingers, unless Tony lost his last match.

My shot differential was better, so while sitting out the bye, I watched Tony take on Brett in the final round. If Brett won by anything less than 21 shots, I would get through the section. If he won by over 21, he would pass us both and take out the section.

Brett won comfortably by about 10 shots, so I qualified for the final on three wins with the best shot differential. In the other pool, Sean Thomas from Queensland had got through undefeated and was my opponent in the National final. This giant of a guy was just 15 and had been playing since he was old enough to walk.

The National final was mostly a blur. My concentration was intense, and my nerves seemed to have subsided. I got off to a good start, consolidating in the middle section of the game, and led 17-11 with just two ends to go. Sean played a great penultimate end, leaving me three and a measure down with one bowl to play. If I failed on this last shot, the game would come down to the last end.

We were on the first of twelve mats, directly under the basketball ring in the stadium. The key section of the court made the mat do some funny things, especially on the backhand towards the grandstand. All the foot traffic from basketball matches made the placement of our mat difficult. It wasn't completely flat like other sections of the floor.

The backhand to the grandstand was only about one-third carpet width for grass-line. This was extremely rare in indoor bowls; normally you would be three-quarter width or more on a flat carpet.

I knew the line I needed for my last bowl had to be tight, or I would hang out and have no impact on the count. The bowl came out slightly under the line I wanted but was still a chance. I remember wanting to reach the counters on the under-side of the head, reducing the count as much as I could. To my excitement, the bowl held its line down the mat, wrested on the pack of counters and fell back on the jack to score one. I jumped with excitement! If someone threw me a basketball, I reckon I would have slam-dunked it through the ring above.

The last end was a non-event being seven shots in front. I would drop a single and claim the 1998 indoor biased bowls National Junior Singles Gold Medal. My first Australian Gold Medal at 16 years of age. I was ecstatic!

I called my parents from the payphone, crying tears of joy as I told them I'd won. I heard Mum and Dad cheering through the phone, proud of their little Australian champ. This was the start of an eight-year State career with Victoria, before I finally quit the game in 2006.

In that period, I won three Victorian Junior State Singles Gold Medals, a State Mixed Pairs Gold Medal, two National Junior Singles Gold Medals, two open National Men's Triples Gold Medals, and probably the biggest achievement of them all, five Victorian Men's Masters Singles Gold Medals.

Indoor bowls taught me the art of singles play and how to cope mentally match by match. I needed to relay this competitiveness and mental toughness onto the bowls green, taking the next big step as a lawn bowler.

I had to become an animal in singles.

I needed to feel the thrill of winning and the pain of losing.

I needed a game plan to match it with the best.

I wanted to feel I could beat anyone, anywhere, one-on-one, in a singles match.

The rest is history.

CHAPTER 14

Carrot

In a tournament with Richard Gale and the charismatic Nick Petrie at Daylesford, I was thrown a carrot to join the all-conquering Altona Bowling Club. After just one season at Footscray Park, I decided it was an offer I couldn't refuse.

Altona was the place to be in Victorian bowls. They were the most successful Premier Division club in the competition and had many State bowlers. Some of these included Mark Jacobsen, who won the Commonwealth Games Pairs Gold Medal that September with Brett Duprez, Nick Petrie, Shane Fordham, Bryce Stewart, Chris Annet, Ian Ewing, and Paul Dorgan, the greatest lawn bowler I ever saw in my lifetime. Not long before, the club also had Mark Casey, Brad Greening, Brendan Egan, and Mark Cowan. The list goes on. They were without doubt, the most star-studded premier division side in the game's history.

In September of 1998, I had a few games on the sand-based synthetic, and then on the grass greens when they opened. I loved the synthetic because I grew up on the stuff at Mount Cottrell. It was also free running, which at the time was better than freshly opened slow grass greens for me.

As a 16-year-old, I was able to play well on the synthetic, but once I hit the grass greens, my inability to play on slow greens was discovered. There was no way I could even consider getting a game in the premier division side until I learnt how to handle slow grass greens.

For the first round of pennant, I was selected in division two, which was Altona's third side. After working hard all week on the slow greens, I was able to play well at Yarraville/Footscray on their grass, even though we were soundly beaten. I had begun putting the heavy green demons behind me.

The next week we played at home and this time, had a great win. I had another decent game, although the slightly quicker Altona greens were much more comfortable for me. By round three, I had made my way into division one, the second side. I enjoyed leading for players such as Bon Deacon, Colin Gee, Doug Grossman, and Neil McKinnon. Even Robert signed at the club before Christmas, and we played together in the same pennant side.

When Robert turned 18 in January, he got a licence, which meant we no longer had to get public transport from Melton to Altona. He was a year and three days older than me, but it would be years yet until I went for my license. His little white Holden Gemini was a beast, but it got us there safely every week.

We made the finals in division one, but unfortunately lost to Yarraville/Footscray at Werribee and were knocked out. The hunger was there for a flag, as we couldn't be promoted. We already had a team in premier division, so a potential flag was our best result possible.

The premier side had a nightmare campaign after finishing clear on top of the ladder. They were upset by Burwood in the double-chance semi-final and then shocked by Burden Park in the preliminary final, knocked out of the Premier Division in straight sets. Burden Park went on to win the flag with the work-horse team, all under the intelligent and thoughtful coaching of Geoff Maskell.

I learnt a lot from my first season at Altona and knew I had to find a couple of extra cogs if I ever wanted to find my way into premier division.

That winter, Robert and I played in the Mount Cottrell winter pennant again. This time we teamed up with Fred Bell and Geoff Marchant from Sunbury. This was a special win for us. After starting together in the competition a few years earlier, we demonstrated we had improved out of sight from the early days, taking home the premiership and prize money.

I also worked very hard on the greens that winter and put down more bowls than I ever had before. Bear in mind that I was in Year 12 at school and trying to get the ENTER score I needed for university.

When the 1999/2000 season started at Altona, I was in preparation for final exams and couldn't devote the time needed on the green. I hadn't done all this schooling to fail at the last hurdle, so bowls took a backseat role for a couple of months.

I studied my arse off. Every day and night I would go through all my school notes, all the course material and learn everything I needed to know back-to-front. I wanted to hit those school exams confidently and ready to get the grades I needed to study Commerce Law at Melbourne University.

My English exam was first, and I smashed it. It would end up an A+ paper and set the tone for what would hopefully be a good week. I followed up with an A+ in further mathematics, an A+ in business management, and an A+ in accounting.

My downfall exams were economics and mathematical methods. Despite reviewing everything we learnt in economics multiple times, two of the five questions on the exam asked for answers I didn't know. I didn't miss a day of school in year 12, so seeing 40% of exam questions that I had no idea about, was very uncomfortable. The fact was, these two elements of economics had not been taught to us by our own teacher, even though I later found out that they were in the course guide.

After leaving the exam room flustered, I went straight to our teacher in his office and piled on a barrage of mouth abuse. I swore blind that if that exam result cost me my university entry score, he would need to look over his shoulder for the rest of his life. I was fuming, devastated and angry. No-one had worked as hard as me in school, but I had no chance answering questions that I had never been taught about.

Mathematical methods only scored me a C+ on my final exam, but this was expected. I took on the extra subject to score bonus ENTER points. You were only scored on five subjects in year 12, with the sixth subject yielding just 10% of its total score. I neglected the subject most of the year, putting most of my efforts into my five main electives. I was confident I could get five A+'s in those.

Economics ended up with a debilitating B. Those two questions I didn't know were clearly why I had scored so badly. I probably aced the three I knew, and hardy scored on the other two.

My ENTER score of 90 was not enough to get my ticket into Commerce Law at Melbourne University. It wasn't even close. To make matters worse, I missed the 94-qualifying score to study Commerce at Melbourne, the same score required for Commerce Law at Deakin University. My first three course choices for university were out of reach. I had to settle for Commerce at Deakin University, a disaster for many reasons.

I lived in Melton and Deakin was in Burwood. I had no license or car. It meant I had a five-hour return trip of buses, trains, and trams daily, for the next three years. On top of that, I would never achieve the law degree I wanted, unless I was willing to study for an extra four years. I did however pass my course with distinction averages, majoring in Commercial Law, Accounting, Finance and Financial Planning. My major highlight was a class-topping score of 98 in Business Tax Law, a subject I found enjoyable and easy to understand.

But for now, back to 1999.

CHAPTER 15

Adult

The selectors were kind enough to leave me in the division one team at Altona, despite not being able to put the time in on the green. Considering my lack of training, I was not too unhappy with the way I was playing.

By round eight, just days after my exams had finished, I was presented with a dream opportunity. I was selected to play second for Shane Fordham in premier division against McKinnon at home. Back in 1999, McKinnon was home to players like Michael Wilks, Todd Simmons, Brad Martin, and Dave Shortall. They were more than a competitive side.

I couldn't have asked for a much better debut, knowing I was still learning a lot about the game. We won comfortably overall and, on our rink, so I was confident of keeping my spot in the side for a few weeks. I played up until Christmas in the same rink, but by then my form had started to struggle.

On the side, after six years of trialling for the Victorian Junior State Side, I was selected for my first series. The only thing that stood between that January series and my State debut, was the millennium bug and potential end to the world.

My attitude toward the end of the world had changed a lot over the previous three years. I wasn't so sure anymore if I wanted the world to end or not. I think this was one of the best times of my life and I was a 17-year-old in my prime. Even though the dreaded gay feelings remained, it didn't control my life anymore. I had somewhat accepted the fact.

Year 2000 arrived without a hitch. No computers blew up, no planes fell out of the sky, and no robots turned on humans to devour the population. The world was just as it was in 1999.

In late January, I joined Barrie Lester, Russell Green Junior, Joel Simmonds, and Michael Walker in the test series against New South Wales at St Johns Park. All five of us would later represent the open men's Victorian team, while three of us would go on to play for Australia. Fair to say it was a handy junior five-a-side at the time.

We won the series 2.5 to 0.5 which included a 30-3 victory in our very first test match in the fours. About to turn 18, it would be my first and last junior test series. I was purely grateful for the opportunity to be honest. Winning the series was just the icing on a delicious cake.

Two weeks later I was an adult.

On a warm Monday morning, I was surprised to learn from Mum and Dad that my first day as an adult would be visiting Crown Casino. I wasn't due for orientation week at university until mid-February, so still had two more weeks of Christmas holidays to enjoy. It was a great idea at the time. Birth Certificate on hand and a bright pink 'I'm 18 today' button hanging from my shirt, we entered the casino. Unfortunately, I needed photo identification, and my birth certificate or student card was not enough to get me through the door. Without a license or Learner's Permit, we were turned away.

Dad completely lost his nut. I could see his Maltese blood flowing through his neck, veins visible for all to see. He sprayed the security guard in only a way a European can. Half his anger was shouted in English, with the other half a classic mix of Maltese swear words. Mum had to grab him and pull him away, otherwise Dad would have spent my birthday in lock-up.

To be honest, it didn't really phase me. We only lost two hours driving there and back, with still the whole afternoon to celebrate. We ended up at the Melton Country Club, where Mum and Dad were life members. I had no issue being let in. All the staff knew I was turning 18 because Mum and Dad had been talking about it to them in the weeks prior.

I tasted my first beer – it was the first alcohol I had ever tried. It never interested me as a teenager, but when turning 18, I was keen to try it. I also had a play on the poker machines in my first try at gambling. It was an exciting day experiencing 'adult' things for the first time. After an awesome home-cooked dinner that night, I called it a day.

Not long asleep, I woke in a pile of sweat, heart-racing, and feeling sick. I tried to dismiss it as the affects of a few beers and a big day, flipping back over to try and sleep.

I couldn't stand the overwhelming feelings that came over me. I jumped out of bed and ran to the bathroom. My head was light, like a balloon, and I was very dizzy. It was like in that moment, I left my own body, floating above and looking down on myself. For someone who had never missed a day of school through illness, had never really been sick, it was a shock to my mind and body.

I jammed a couple of fingers down my throat to throw up in the basin. I wasn't even thinking at the time. It was like I was in a trance, surviving on autopilot. Despite dry reaching a couple of times, I couldn't bring anything up. My heart was pounding like a drum in my chest and constant bursts of pins and needles were felt from head to toe. It was like I was burning up, yet I was shaking and freezing cold. It was then I started to panic.

I bolted to Mum and Dad's room and bashed on their bedroom door hard. Mum woke up and spoke to me through the door. I could hardly speak, quivering on the tiled floor. Dad heard my mumbles and showing his own concern, got out of bed and came to my aide.

He sat me down for a couple of minutes, asking me questions about what I was feeling. Mum also got out of bed and came to see how I was doing. It was hard to describe what I was feeling to them.

I wanted to spew my guts up, but nothing was there.

I wanted to get up and walk, but my legs were now jelly.

I wanted to speak to Mum and Dad, but I was breathing so fast, no words would come out.

I wanted to know why I was feeling this way, but no-one had any answers.

With serious concern, Mum called an ambulance. I sat there on the couch staring at the clock, rocking back and forth to the sound of the seconds hand ticking. It took less than five minutes for the paramedics to arrive and straight away, they were concerned by my severe sweating, pale-white face, and the uncontrollable shaking I had from head to toe.

They took my vitals. Oxygen was perfect, but my heart rate was in the low 200's. I hadn't been exercising or running around, so a heart rate that high was abnormal. Once the vital signs were all checked, it was concluded by the paramedics that I was experiencing an attack of anxiety, a reasonably common thing to happen to people of all ages.

The paramedics helped me up off the couch and assisted me in slowly walking around the room, trying to lower my heart rate. Despite feeling terrible, I was comforted by the fact that I had both professional help, and my parents were with me. After ten minutes or so, my heart rate began to slow down, and the paramedics saw it as their time to leave. They said I should go and walk around the block slowly a couple of times and that my heart rate should return to normal.

Strangely enough, I felt comfortable enough to go outside alone and take a walk. I walked around the block no less than five times, taking well over three hours to complete. My heart rate had slowed down, I felt at peace, and I could go back home to bed.

I wrote the attack down as a one-off event at the time, believing it may have been caused by the alcohol and a huge day out. I was hopeful that it was a scare I would never have to experience again. Without over-exaggerating, for someone who had never been sick before, it felt like I was about to curl up and die. I tried to forget about it, but my elephant-like memory wouldn't let go.

It was always in the back of my mind.

CHAPTER 16

Uni

From what I had heard about university and from what I saw on television at the time, this was supposed to be the greatest time of my life. There was alcohol, sex, drugs, and partying like never before. It was a period of experimentation and life lessons, or so I thought.

A normal day of university for me was a 4:14am alarm (because that's the time of the morning I was born), a black coffee and quick scrub, followed by a 40-minute walk to Melton train station. The buses didn't run that early, so to make an 8:00am lecture, I had to get to the station by foot for the 5:21am service to Southern Cross Station. Arriving shortly after 6:00am, I had a five-minute walk to the tram stop. There, I would catch the number 75 to Deakin in Burwood. It was more than 60 stops and in traffic, could take an hour and a half easily. My tram was so early that I often missed the traffic and peak-hour commuters, getting to Burwood by about

7:10am. Should I miss my early morning train from Melton, the next train wouldn't get me to university on time.

After a few hours of lectures and tutorials, I would catch the tram back to Southern Cross station for my train back to Melton. If I just missed a train, I would sometimes have to wait over an hour for the next service. At least now, once in Melton, there was a bus service to take me home. Generally, I'd be home after dinner time and reheat mine in the microwave before heading to bed and repeating the dose the following day.

If I had to train for bowls, I would get off the number 75 at Flinders Street Station and catch the train to Altona on the Werribee line. When training was done, I would catch the train back to Flinders Street but get off at Footscray. From there I could meet the train to Melton, saving me go all the way back into the city. These nights, normally being Thursdays, I wouldn't get home any time before 9:00pm.

For the most part of three years I did this. It is no wonder I burnt out in my early 20's.

I was a total nerd with studies and didn't know a soul at Deakin. Not one of my school mates even got close to the ENTER score needed to qualify for a course there. As like the day I first started high school, I was confronted by a concrete jungle of buildings and hundreds of faces I didn't know.

'O-week' was supposed to help the transition of newbies from high school into university, but it did nothing for me. I didn't speak to anyone for the whole week I visited. I just followed the tour guides around, learning my way through the epic campus. By the end of the week, I gained enough courage to try the university café and order a coffee. I had never had a fancy coffee before. I only drank black instant coffee at home, so had no idea what to order. I ended up ordering a short-black, thinking it was a black coffee in a small-sized cup. I didn't want a whole mug full of coffee that time of day. To my dismay, I ended up with a dribble of coffee in a cup so strong, I couldn't even smell it let alone drink it. Lesson learnt.

University was a serious challenge, especially one as well-renowned as Deakin. For the first time ever in my education, I was struggling to keep up. Between the long travel hours, reading hundreds of pages of text, completing weekly exercises for tutorials and sitting through two-hour lectures, my interest in the 'further education' concept was fading fast.

It was the group assignments that helped me find friends at university. It was an uncomfortable experience nonetheless, as I had never completed a group assignment before. I was a perfectionist, so didn't accept lacklustre efforts from teammates. I often ended up doing the whole assignment by myself and improving the work of other group members. This disgruntled my group, to such a point that they sometimes complained to the lecturer. I was so confident and arrogant that I would dismiss any ideas the team had that contradicted my own thoughts.

After receiving correspondence from more than one lecturer, I decided to take a backseat role in future assignments and leave the majority up to the team. To my surprise, these kids knew more about the subjects than I did. It was hard to come from a high school of so many strugglers, to an environment where people were more intelligent than me. I had to learn to trust my team. My eyes were opening to a bigger and brighter world.

I got through most of my subjects in year one but struggled with the economics subjects. It's hard to believe that the simplest rules and theories were often the hardest for me to understand. I could give you a lecture on Marxism or Capitalism but would struggle to describe the theories of scarce resources and demand and supply. My mind was outside the realm of basic rules, so my first year of university was the hardest. Eventually I learnt that the understanding of these base concepts would expand and grow in the next two years of studies, and without knowing them, a student would ultimately fail.

In eight subjects over two semesters, I scored only two high distinctions. These results were hard to swallow for someone who was used to scoring nothing but the best. It did wake me though. I had to work harder in the future to make the scores.

The major positive of the year was not having to repeat any units. Some of my friends didn't pass units, meaning their course would stretch to a fourth year before graduating.

During that first semester, I played in the division one side at Altona after being dropped post-Christmas. This was fine by me, as my form before the break wasn't up to standard.

I played the year out, thinking my opportunity to play premier division had been lost. Bryce Stewart called me one Wednesday night leading into the finals and told me that I had been selected as second for him in the first final against Burwood at MCC. I was in total shock. He was third in our rink before Christmas, and I wasn't setting the world on fire in any regard. And yet, he was willing to take me on as his second in some of the biggest games in club history. Maybe he saw something in me that few others noticed at the time.

We beat Burwood and I had a decent game, setting up a grand final berth against Melbourne at Ringwood. That was a very black day in my bowls career. It must have been close to the worst game of pennant I ever played, along with many of our players. We arrived late on the bus, rushed onto the green, never performed, and got smashed off the park on stodgy 11-second track. It was a 30-shot demolition by Melbourne, leaving a very bitter taste in my mouth. Two years without a Premiership for that Altona side was unbelievable, knowing the quality they fielded every week.

The highlight of the season for me was being selected in the State Pennant side to play at Corowa. In those days, the eight country region winners as well as the Metropolitan premier division winner and runner-up, were the ten invited teams. I was leading for Bryce Stewart. Here was a bloke who had given me more chances than I deserved, willing to take me into battle again after my string of failures.

I had broken a finger in my left hand the week before, playing football with some friends. It needed a splint and bandage, as well as pain killers. Thankfully I was right-handed, so it had little influence on my bowling. For five section matches and the final, I was able to finally provide my team with some close bowls. The free-running greens at Corowa put me back in my comfort zone, leading as good as anyone in the tournament.

The final against Melbourne was semi-revenge for our grand final disaster. Although a reasonably tight finish, we got over the line and won the State Pennant. It gave us something to build on before premier division started again in October.

By the time university had wrapped up in early November, I was already leading in the premier division side that next season. Bryce took a coaching job in Port Macquarie and my new skipper was Paul 'Pebbles' Dorgan.

At home, things weren't so great. I got in a big argument with my parents and threatened to move out. I always thought I'd live at home until 30, but things changed very quickly. As a hot-headed young adult, I stuck by my word and left.

Three weeks later I moved into a share house in Altona, around the corner from the bowling club. Mum and Dad couldn't believe I left, but the separation only brought us closer together over time.

I was on Youth Allowance and not working, so I had to be very careful with money. Being close to the club, I could put in extra time on the green. I was also closer to university for the time being and shortened my return trip by two hours each day.

Life, as like bowls, is always more successful when given opportunity. In terms of bowls for me, it all comes back to one man. The one who was willing to cop the rap of my selection and the risk of me failing yet again. The man, who at the time was the biggest influence on my bowling career. The single person who put his own arse on the line purely for my benefit.

I will never forget the start you gave me.

Thank You, Bryce Stewart.

CHAPTER 17

Shift

When Robert moved in with us at the Altona share house, I started to have problems there. Our friendship was thinning, and we were arguing every time we saw each other. The last straw was when he punched a hole in my bedroom door. I had to get out of there.

My Pop was battling illness in hospital and his unit in Melton was available for house sitting. Living alone was something I had never done before, but with Mum and Dad around the corner and other family nearby, I was crazy if I didn't take up the free rent. After just a few months in Altona, I was back in Melton experiencing that five-hour return trip from university again.

As winter approached, I set my focus on the Junior Australian Singles for indoor bowls. I had turned 18 already, but the age threshold was under-19. After a poor performance in Adelaide in 1999, I was determined to make amends in my home State.

My delivery had gone to water. I hadn't put the work in I needed to and began developing a horrible backhand wobble on the bowl. I had the 'yips' completely on my backhand and avoided it as much as possible during the Nationals.

Playing one-handed, I got through my pool, but it was a titanic struggle. I beat Matt Cameron before losing yet again to my Queensland nemesis Tony Williams. Needing to win my last two games, I got past Owen Wraight from New South Wales, and then put on a short-end masterclass of 'forehand around the clock' against Josh Tegg from Tasmania. I was in the final.

It was freezing in Ballarat. We would often start the mornings with coats of ice on the mats, watching it melt away under the power of the jet heaters. I swore it snowed that week. I don't think the temperature reached double-figures once the whole time we were there.

The National final was a fairytale for me. With close family and friends watching on, I took on a young Shawn Armstrong from Tasmania, who had bolted the other section in. Shawn was only 12 years old at the time but would later go on to win numerous National titles and play for Australia. He is still rated as one of the top players in the country today.

I won the first nine ends of the contest to lead 14-0 and from there, it was party time. With a final scoreline of 28-6 after the 21 ends of play, it became the biggest winning margin of any National indoor biased bowls final up to that point. I was thrilled to win it a second time and join and illustrious list of two-time champions. In the grandstand, Shawn was crying in his dad's arms after the defeat.

Over the past few years, Shawn and I have caught up through *facebook* and rekindled an old friendship. I have been down to Tasmania a couple of times to see him and catch up on everything. We enjoy a few drinks, a game of bowls, and one of the ultimate pleasures in life; talking absolute garbage! I often remind him about his crying performance in Ballarat. Even his dad, Anthony, has a chuckle with him about it too. Probably a bit rough on a kid who was 12 at the time, but funny now.

Coming back down the Western Highway home that night, I couldn't help but stare at the enormous trophy and beautiful gold pin. It was sensible tactics and a massive hunger for winning that got me through those championships. Understanding that I had shortfalls, I developed a game plan that allowed me to play to my strengths. From that point on, I began taking notes on games and tournaments, learning what worked best for me. It was the starting point for one of my books 'In the Zone – Developing Mental Toughness in Bowls'.

With the indoor season done and dusted, it was time to hit the greens for a third year at Altona. I had earned a few brownie points after playing well in the State Pennant winning side and was rewarded with a lead spot in the Premier Division.

After a handful of games, I was moved over to Paul Dorgan's rink, where I would stay for the remainder of the season. We had some massive wins as a rink and only a couple of little losses. It was during my games with Paul that I realised he was one of the best, if not the best, player I had ever seen. His touch draw bowls, thunderous forehand drives, and his placid nature on the green made him great to play with. Those big size five 'bombs' produced shots that only 'Pebbles' could. He was nicknamed 'Zig-Zag' because even his off target drives seemed to bounce left and right off a handful of bowls and still produce the magic result. It's probably what made him so great. Skipping is about getting results. There are no pictures on the scorecard.

With the previous two years yielding no premiership, the true Altona style returned for that finals campaign. After a comfortable double-chance semi final win against Melbourne, we replayed them in the grand final at Yarraville/Footscray. I think we got up by about 12 shots overall in the end, but we were never challenged. The margin was comfortable all game long. The 'gold flag' was also my first ever pennant premiership as a bowler. A premiership is something you never get sick of winning. The more you win, the more you want. It's addictive.

I was now 19, in my second year of university, had played for Victoria in junior bowls and now won a premier division flag. I was wondering what else I could do to improve my game. After quiet discussions with players at Altona, I was given the impression that

I would lead for another year or two before moving up the playing positions. Both Russell Green Junior and Joel Simmonds had made the Open Victorian Men's team that year, and this became my new goal. I had to win something major. I had to do it quickly.

It was possible that I could make the State team by playing at Altona. I was surrounded by current State players, and being seen with the best bowlers, was always an advantage when it came to selection. I also had the potential opportunity of entering State championships with some of these players, hoping to win that elusive title and get noticed. I wasn't going to make any decisions on my playing future until after the indoor season.

With the dreaded backhand wobble still floating around, I somehow managed to produce good results at the State championships and the State trials. For that reason, I was selected to play the Men's Singles for Victoria, just one year out of the juniors.

I had a very winnable section, but the wobble was affecting my confidence and had even started appearing on my favoured forehand. I had one win and one draw out of four games which is nothing to be ashamed of, but the opportunity to make an open National final at just 19 had gone begging. Then, and now, I am still the youngest player ever selected to play singles for their State at open level. That is something I can hang my hat on at least. The men were a different class to the boys, and realistically, I was still just a boy.

By winter's end, university exams were close and major studying was required. I got invited to the Victorian State under-25 trials, which I wasn't going to miss, so for one weekend I took some time away from my books.

I was leading for Graeme Venables, with Mathew Kurta third, and Luke Aiello second. Luke and Mathew were two of the funniest blokes you could ever meet. They both had a huge fire to win, but their joke-cracking and funny stories had me in stitches of laughter. We struck an instant friendship that continues today, even though we have grown-up, we created memories of a lifetime.

It's funny how it all works out sometimes. After a weekend of fun, drinks, and conversation, they had convinced me to join the freight-train that was Bundoora. They reminded me that bowls was a competitive sport, but just a sport. Sport was for fun and these guys knew how to do that. It opened my eyes to a broader world of what bowls could really be.

It was a lifestyle, not a chore.

I lived in Melton, went to university in Burwood, and was now a bowling member at Bundoora – all with no licence or car.

What the hell was I thinking?

CHAPTER 18

Bundy

Bundoora was an awesome club to me. They were full of guys my age, and I was about to start a six-year stint that would lift my bowls career to new heights.

The club's top grade was only in division one, but that wasn't a concern to me. It became a place where I could play a reasonably high level of bowls, play with new mates, and enjoy a social life outside of the club.

Leaving Altona wasn't an easy decision. I had everything there on a platter and for some reason, thought it was a good idea to leave it all behind. The best players in the State were there and I was learning at a supersonic speed. Many of them told me I was crazy to go; they were probably right. It was a risky play that would see me either disappear into the bowls abyss or make a positive stance on the sport. Being my fourth club in just eight years, I already had the reputation of a 'club-jumper', so this move had to be a long stay.

Along with Mathew and Luke, Bundoora had Adam Galloway and Brent Reiner. One year later, Nick McIntyre would return and the famous five was formed.

The first practice match in September was unforgettable for all the wrong reasons. We played Montmorency on their sand-based synthetic, a division two club that was always competitive at home. I played third for Adam Galloway, in a full-strength Bundoora outfit. We were annihilated overall and, on our rink, losing by about 70 shots in total. It left us red-faced and completely down on confidence.

What had I done?

What had I got myself into?

Could this club play or what?

Luke was an intelligent mind around bowls. He told me that Montmorency were in a class of their own at home on their fast synthetic and that I shouldn't read too much into it. It was a scary thought though, to be smashed by a division two club in that fashion. But Luke was right, and things were about to turn for the better.

We played the section favourites, Dandenong Club, in round one on their grass. In a tight tussle, we went down by half a dozen shots to a very good side. We came out of the game with a lot more positives than negatives, understanding that they were the benchmark in our section. This gave us enough belief that we could win a few games before Christmas and ensure we were safely out of the relegation zone.

That first night after pennant, I stayed at Luke's house after we hit the beers at the club. I wasn't a big drinker, so it didn't take me much to get plastered. I was as drunk as I had ever been, and I felt the pain on Sunday. I kept jumping out of bed that night running to the bathroom in anticipation of throwing up. Just to be on the safe side, I spent much of the night there and outside with their dog 'Zac', not wanting to soil the house on my first night's stay.

That week, Luke called to tell me there were no changes to the side. He also told me to get down to the club Thursday night, as the leadership group had decided to play all our home games on the synthetic green. Bells started ringing in my head, wondering if leaving Altona to play on synthetic in a lower grade was really the best thing for me. Just a month earlier, we had been whacked on a similar green at Montmorency and suddenly, we were taking a punt to use our own artificial surface. Fair to say that I didn't agree with the decision at the time, but who was I to doubt the club leaders. I was a newbie and had to do what I was told.

In a great performance, we beat Footscray Park by over 50 shots with all rinks up. Getting our first win was a priority, but to do it in that style was fantastic for the club. I couldn't believe that the synthetic move paid off. If we continued to play like that at home, we would take some serious beating.

Bundoora piled on six more wins, before a shock loss to last-placed Sunshine City in round nine. It made our round ten match against Dandenong Club at home, crucial to the section standings. We would win that game all rinks up and take top spot on the table.

I won my first club singles title that December, beating club legend Keith Deveson in the final. John McIntyre and I also won the region pairs title, and I made the State finals of the Under 25 singles. I would win three of those finals to progress to the State final, which back then was played on premier division grand final day. I also got through the region Champion of Champions Singles and landed a final 16 spot at Trafalgar in April.

After Christmas, we kept winning pennant matches and formed such a gap at the top of the ladder, that finals were on the cards. By season end, we had earned the top rank qualifying spot of the four sections and earned a double-chance.

We played Sunbury at Burwood, with the winner to progress to the division one grand final and earn a promotion to premier division. Mathew Kurta played a game to remember, scoring a big rink win over Mark Cowan. Other rinks did their jobs and at 29 shots in front with three ends to go, both clubs shook hands. Bundoora made the grand final and were also promoted into premier division.

Two weeks later we met Sunbury in the grand final after they knocked out Altona's number two side in the preliminary final. With both teams already qualifying for premier division, most saw the chance to win a flag as a bonus. I disagreed. When given the opportunity of a flag, you needed to grab it with both hands. Forty teams started in division one and only two remained. This was a classic opportunity to score a white flag, even after being rank outsiders at the start of the season.

The final was a non-event on a very slippery Keilor surface. We won our rink by 28 against Alan Langley, while others did their job in a 41-shot demolition of Sunbury. Bundoora were division one champions, and I started to feel a lot better about my decision to move there. The only thing that would top the weekend off, was to win the Under 25 State Singles the next day against Barrie Lester at Yarraville/Footscray.

A reasonably quiet night ensued, before trekking to Yarraville/Footscray the following morning. I was a clear under-dog in the match, with Barrie recently making the Victorian Men's State Side as a lead. I felt I was certainly a chance to win the match but had to play a great game to do it.

Melbourne and Altona were going hammer and tong in the premier division final, their third straight year against each other. Just 12 months earlier, I was donning the Altona shirt and winning the flag with them. Now, I was a division one premiership winner, dressed up in Bundoora gear, playing a match on the same green as my ex-teammates.

With the big match in the centre of the green, Barrie and I were wedged up against the grandstand on a ditch rink. The green was very two-paced, and the wind was totally unpredictable and frustrating. The match was never going to be pretty, but with a State title on the line, there would be fireworks. It was all about playing the big bowls when required and making the most out of favourable heads.

After two and a half hours of draw-shot play, we found ourselves locked at 23-all. The premier division half time bell had gone, but none of the Altona or Melbourne players went inside. They were all standing around watching our game, transfixed on what would be the last eight bowls of the match.

Lying two down with one bowl to play, I had to make a very tough decision. I could attempt to draw the shot to lead 24-23 and risk losing the match if I failed or play a forehand runner to remove one of Barrie's bowls or kill the end.

After looking closely at the head, I decided to run at Barrie's closest bowl. If I was a bowl narrow, I would get the jack, while one bowl wide would at least take out his second shot and I would save the match. It's funny how things happen in bowls. I must have told this story 1,000 times over the years and it always puts a smile on my face. It became a magic moment in my bowling memory bank.

I let my runner go and it appeared to be on the high side of Barrie's shot bowl. Watching the bowl go down the green was like looking at a video in slow-motion. For a long time, I thought I might get the tiny gap between his two bowls and fail. Seeing my runner clip his second shot out was a relief, but to see it deflect and take out his other shot bowl also, was unbelievable. The dust settled and two of my green-ringed ABT2000 bowls that were previously third and fourth shots, were now the only two bowls in sight. Before anyone could soak up what had just happened, I was already in the grandstand jumping up and down with my Bundoora teammates. I must have been there for over a minute, only to turn around and see Barrie and the marker, the legendary Robert Middleton, still stationary and in shock from what had just happened.

Handshakes were the order of the day, and I was presented with the Brad Greening trophy.

That night, I was interviewed by Robert Middleton on the radio about the match. I was also asked why I decided to leave Altona, after seeing them win yet another flag against Melbourne the same day. For the first time, I was being noticed in lawn bowls. I was no longer a small fish in a big pond. My dream of playing for Victoria was fast becoming a reality.

At Trafalgar Bowls Club, the State Champion of Champions singles was a decent run. I won through to the semi-final where I met a singles master, Mulgrave's John Leitch.

On a sub-13 second green, John threw ditch-to-ditch jack lengths at me, while I threw short ends back at him when I was in control of the mat. Leitch had just beaten Mark Jacobsen in his quarterfinal the day before, so I knew the match was going to be tough. In a marathon that lasted over three hours and 42 live ends, Leitch proved a little too good, knocking me out 25-22. He then went on to beat Todd Simmons in the final and become the State Champion of Champions singles winner.

That match against Leitch had a massive influence on the way I played singles moving forward. I believed his style of play was so simple, yet so genius. He threw long ends and nailed his draw bowls. Every time he put his first bowl on the jack, I found it hard to win the end. One tiny gust of wind or one imperfection in the green was enough to fail over that distance. It was also hard to convert over that length, or to hit single bowl targets when driving. On shorter ends, he was very aggressive. He used his quality runners to literally drive me off the green. His theory was to out-draw his opponents on long ends, while on shorter lengths, he would back his aggressive game. I liked it, so I started doing it myself.

If I wanted to take the next step in singles, I had to adopt this game plan. I needed a plan that could get me through multiple singles matches in a row. After all, you need to win about 15 games straight to win the State Champion of Champions singles.

I modelled my singles training on that style, working hard over the winter on ditch-to-ditch draw bowls and accurate short end hitting. My game would take a step or two backwards in the next 12 months, but it was short-term pain for a long-term gain. I was positive that I could eventually master that style of play and develop a singles game that would win me many more games.

So, ditch-to-ditch it was.

CHAPTER 19

Mortarboard

While training my new style of game that winter on the weekends, I spent all my spare time studying for final year university exams. To help with much needed income, I started a job calling bingo in Brunswick. I'd go to university during the day, study while travelling, then call bingo in the evening. I got the last train home to Melton after work and would walk from the station back to Pop's unit. On the nights I worked, I'd only get about four hours sleep before my dreaded 4:14am alarm would start singing. It was a tough time on my mind and body. I had plans and expectations, but they would come with stress and fatigue.

Our premier division season began in October, just weeks before my final exams. I wasn't training during the week due to study and work, so I felt under-prepared for the season to come. Couple this with trying to find work placement after graduation, and you can understand the pressure I was under. Even once found, the financial burden of buying a few suits, shirts, and ties, would be a massive problem for someone with barely any money. Bowls became a hassle and a chore, taking up time I needed for more important issues.

My hard work paid off. I finished my final semester of university with three high distinctions and a distinction, earning graduation as a Bachelor of Commerce with majors in Commercial Law, Accounting, Finance, and Financial Planning, or in fancy terms, a BCom(A.F.FP.CL). 16 years of continuous education was over, and it was time to hit the professional workforce.

I found a job as a File Accountant at Worrells in the Melbourne CBD, a boutique accounting firm specialising in Bankruptcy and Corporate Insolvency. This was the perfect opportunity to combine my knowledge of accounting and commercial law, with skills in both of those areas required when working in insolvency. With plans to start during the first week of February 2003, I could get my focus back on bowls and planning for my 21st birthday in January.

After exams were done, I visited my Pop in Broadmeadows hospital, hearing he wasn't doing well. He had been fighting illness for over a year and had become very frail. Mum had visited him earlier that morning and suggested I should go and see him before it was too late. His memory was going, so I brought in some old photos from his unit of his days on the tramways. His eyes lit up with the photos of old trams, the South Melbourne Depot, and his old work colleagues. He knew every tram model, every number for every route, and the names of everyone he worked with.

I thought he was doing better than everyone was suggesting. In a particularly sad moment, he asked me when Mum was going to come and visit him. He had already forgotten that Mum was there just hours before, and this was the moment I knew he was battling. I spoke to the nurse privately, and she said that the past few nights he had been getting out of bed and waiting at his door for the 'number one tram from East Coburg to South Melbourne Beach' so that he could go home to Albert Park. He hadn't lived in Albert Park since the mid 90's when he relocated to Melton, so this was especially upsetting to hear.

After an hour or so, he seemed a little flustered and tired, so I left to let him sleep. I was deeply moved that day by the whole concept of life. I wanted to remember my Pop for the great times, not the sickness that threatened to take him away from us. So, I left with only positive thoughts, hoping things might turn around for him.

Later that week, I got a shock phone call from my future boss. He wanted me to start work immediately. It was only early-November when University finished, so there was no decent break before entering the workforce. It was virtually straight from exams to the office, and my life as an insolvency accountant began.

I started work on 11th November, startled by how different it was from university. It would take me weeks before I settled in, but I knew I had to start somewhere. The daunting prospect of working for the next 45 years allowed me to realise there was plenty of time to get things right.

On Sunday 17th of November, my mobile phone rang at 11:20am. I was having brunch at the Bundoora Hotel to celebrate my first completed week of working full-time. I didn't answer the call, but after it rang two more times, I thought I better take it.

My perfect little life vanished before my eyes. It was like the sun went down the moment it came up. My mind was racing, and I began to feel physically ill. Mum told me that my Pop, James Dowel, had passed away that morning in Broadmeadows Hospital. It was a total kick in the guts.

I ran outside with my phone in case I started crying. I know that grandparents always maintain they love their grandchildren equally, but I knew deep-down that I was definitely his favourite.

We played indoor biased bowls together.

He would happily drive me to bowls when I needed a lift.

He dropped us off at school every morning with Mum, then picked us up in the afternoon while Mum cooked dinner.

He ate dinner with our family every night at the dining table with us kids.

My Pop was the secret of why my bowls was blossoming. If it wasn't for his support through my teenage years, I would never have gotten anywhere in the game. His death devastated me.

On the morning of his funeral, off from work on compassionate leave, I went to Mum and Dad's house to get a lift to Springvale. I spent most of the morning in their backyard, sitting on the garden swing crying. No one that close to me had ever died before and I didn't know how to deal with such grief. Dad realised I was suffering and came outside to comfort me. He said a lot of great things about Pop, but all this did was make me feel an even greater loss.

His request before passing was for his seven grandsons to be the pall bearers of his coffin. The service was beautiful as expected, with Aunty Pam, his eldest child, doing his eulogy. She told many great stories of his life, including his huge triangular tower of empty VB long necks that lived in the backyard of his old Albert Park address. Like times when the football would clip a bottle and the enormous structure would come smashing to the ground in a pile of shattered glass. How he would run outside waving his fist in the air and yelling at us. I can't remember if I was laughing or crying at the time – maybe it was both.

When it came time to carry the coffin to the hearse, I was completely overwhelmed with emotion. I wouldn't say that I regretted not taking part, more so disappointed that I didn't have the willpower to do it. I was in a faint-like trance, struggling to stand on my own two feet. I just walked alongside my other six cousins and Pop, as he was carried outside.

He was buried in Springvale cemetery, in the same plot as his wife who died at a young age from cancer in 1984. He had been separated from her for 18 years and as his health deteriorated, he would often say that it was time to be with his beloved Lorraine. A love story cut short in the 1980's was about to be reunited forever in the lawn of Springvale Necropolis. It was a beautiful moment seeing them joined together once again. As the coffin lowered, we said our final goodbyes, turned and walked away. I had tears running down my face, trying to accept the harsh reality that I would never see him again.

He was gone.

I rarely visit the plot nowadays, as I still struggle with his loss even after 20 years. I'd like to go more often, but it isn't something I can do alone. There is still so much emotion inside me. The hole in my heart could never be filled again. Even the passage of time would leave the open wound untreated.

For several years, Pop stayed in my mind through bowls, work, and life. I would always feel his support on my right shoulder. Whether intended or not, he gave me unconditional love in both life and death, and I missed him dearly.

I still do.

Bundoora was struggling to hold on in the premier division, with any win treated like gold. Our goal was to survive in the premier division in our first year, but we were far from safe. We had two 'heat-outs' at home prior to Christmas (when the temperature exceeds 38 degrees) that cost us valuable points, so by Christmas, we were lamenting in a disappointing ninth.

Just two weeks after losing Pop, Dad telephoned me to tell me that my other Pop Jim, had taken ill and was in hospital. For the whole family, it was a lot to take in. His battle was short and on the 12th of December, just four weeks after Pop died, my other Pop Jim Brown passed away.

Nan was inconsolable at the time. Her life was a tough story from day one, growing up in Malta with her blind mother and no father. She left school at ten years of age to become her mum's carer, before moving to Australia in later years after her death. My father's father died at a young age from Huntington's disease before Nan remarried some years later. Her two daughters also had Huntington's Disease and even after losing her second husband, she faced many tough challenges ahead.

She would later bury her two daughters from the dreaded disease and become carer of my cousin Luke, her grandchild, who too had Huntington's disease. What a tough and mighty woman she was to deal with so much pain in her life, and still put family first. She was a survivor.

Christmas came and went, with the two family deaths making it a placid and underwhelming season of festivities. In between all the stresses that had arisen, work continued to go well. I had no issues waking up at 6:00am, suiting up, enjoying a big breakfast and jumping on the train from Melton to Southern Cross. I was on an entry-level salary as a graduate, but I had never seen this sort of money before. I felt like a millionaire.

Despite all the sadness I had been through, as a 20-year-old young male, I had to try and get on with my life. We may have been battling a bit in bowls and suffered family tragedies, but everything else seemed to be falling in to place. My family was closer than ever, work was enjoyable, finances were strong, and I had never felt so comfortable in my own skin. My 21st birthday was close, and it was time to celebrate a milestone and lift ourselves from the grief that had stricken us all.

In January, I got notice to move out of Pop's unit in Melton that I was house-sitting. His deceased estate was with the Trustee who had to realise and distribute his assets in accordance with his last will and testament. I'd have to move out shortly after my birthday.

It was house-hunting time.

CHAPTER 20

Key

After beating Altona by a solitary shot on the first day of February, Bundoora escaped the relegation zone in premier division for the time being, sneaking a couple of points above ninth and tenth place. The result was perfect timing for me. I had turned 21 the day before and my party was set for that Saturday night.

Crammed up in the garage at my Pop's unit, I put on the booze, food, and music, in a celebration of 21 years well-lived. The music echoed loudly in the brick garage, with photos of my younger days taped to the sidewall. I was quite emotional making the speech, labelling my father as a massive influence on my life. Not only had he saved me from death more than once, but he also became the father figure around the house that we so desperately needed. Mum and Dad had been married 12 years by this stage and their relationship was beyond amazing. My parents were the best people in the world.

The night ended reasonably early. Most of my guests had to travel back to Bundoora and were exhausted from the thriller against Altona. I still have my 21st birthday key in a box at the back of my wardrobe. Whenever I want to remember life in its prime, I grab it out and read the friendly messages. A simple smile can change my whole mood when I am down.

With the party done and dusted, I had just three weeks to vacate the unit.

Moving house is a stressful experience at any time. I got lucky with my new house search. A friend of mine knew an old couple in Bundoora who had an empty bungalow at the back of their property in Morwell Avenue. With bowls at Bundoora, most of my friends out there, half the distance to travel to work, and a cheap rent of $520 a month, it seemed like the best option for me at the time.

The move happened so quick that I never really remember it, other than my work mates helped with the truck and belongings. It was the third time I had moved in as many years, so I was familiar with how it all went. I had just got my 'P-plates' and bought a Toyota Cressida GLX, so having wheels was a luxury I never had before. I started as a very nervous driver, especially changing lanes at high speed, but as I got more experienced, the nervousness thinned.

Bundoora survived in premier division with a washout in the final round against Werribee, enough to see us finish seventh. This was easily my best bowls success of the year. I had failed to defend my club singles title, failed to defend my State Under 25 singles title, and had generally performed poorly in all region and state events.

John McIntyre and I did manage to defend our region pairs title but were knocked out in the last 16 of the State at Ringwood. Holding match with a bowl to play, our opponent cleared out the shot bowl clean as a whistle and sent us packing. Our opposition, Glen McGregor and Trevor Stevens, would then go on to win the whole competition and claim the State pairs title.

With the summer season done, my life focused on work. I played once or twice a week on the indoor mats, but certainly didn't put the training time in that I used to. Despite that, I still managed to make the State side as a lead in the Men's triples with Arthur Finch and Glenn Sargent. The wobble that destroyed my game for many years before had somehow vanished, allowing me to lead up well for the team.

By winning the first seven matches at the National championships in Caloundra, and results around us falling our way, we had wrapped up the National gold medal with two rounds still to play. It was so enjoyable playing the last two games knowing we had already won the title. Everyone else was fighting like mad to grab the silver medal, while we were just enjoying the ride.

That win was my third National title in five years on the mats, so I started to think about higher representation. The Trans-Tasman was played against New Zealand every two years and nominations would be called for at the next National championships. The 2004 championships were set for Adelaide, but I never played, so that opportunity was missed.

By September, my third season at Bundoora was imminent. I had received a pay-rise at work along with a promotion. I had even found online sites where I could meet other young guys to explore my sexuality. Life at that very moment was simply perfect.

Nothing could stop me now.

CHAPTER 21

Darkest

WARNING: *This chapter contains profanities and serious issues relating to mental health, suicide, depression, and anxiety, that may offend some readers. Discretion and sensitivity are advised.*

As an intelligent young man, I was confident and arrogant in everything I did. To think work was flourishing was an understatement. I had taken a preference to personal insolvency and my boss had entrusted me with managing two of the highest-profile Bankruptcies of the era. These huge achievements at work had stretched its way to the bowling green where I had just been selected to play for Victoria in the Under 25 side. I had even started skipping in premier division for Bundoora, with our team sitting on the fringe of the final four leading into Christmas.

I spent Christmas in Melton with family, enjoying a much more festive season than the year prior. As usual, everyone was very generous with their gifts to each other. Mum would throw on a Christmas feast of roasts for lunch, and then we would enjoy the cold meats with salad for dinner. Mum made the best salads. Her cauliflower salad was so outstanding, that I managed to get her recipe so I could make it at home.

Driving home to Bundoora on Boxing Day 2003, my life would change forever.

Between Keilor and the Western Ring Road turn off, I started feeling violently ill and dizzy, so had to pull the car over in the emergency lane.

I wanted to spew my guts up, but nothing was there.

I wanted to get up and walk, but my legs were like jelly.

I was breathing so fast that I could feel my heart about to shatter my ribcage.

I wanted to know why I was feeling this way.

Oh, I've been here before. It was the same feelings I had the night I turned 18. I knew exactly what was happening, almost four years to the day I experienced my last anxiety attack. This one was far worse than last time.

I was woken on the side of the road by a young woman shaking me by the collar of my polo shirt. Standing behind her were five or six other motorists who had pulled over to see what was going on. My head was wet, and I was shivering, even though it was easily over 30 degrees. I wasn't sure what was happening. My car was still in park, driver door open and engine still running, while I lay on the ground next to it surrounded by strangers.

No-one had any answers for me when I asked what was going on. I could only assume that I had fainted or passed out. My wet head was blood, and I had a throbbing headache. The nice woman who was comforting me had called an ambulance, which arrived shortly after and took me to hospital. I never knew who these people were, but I am indebted to them. For all I knew, they might have saved me from being run over, seriously injured, or even killed.

I was given six stitches in the top of my head. I was very groggy and tired. I had never fainted or passed out before, so this was a scary experience for me.

Mum and Dad never knew what happened that day because I never told them. They already had enough on their plates. I was a very private person and any dent in my bullet-proof appearance, was to stay purely with me. Whatever this was, I planned to fight it alone.

After about 20 questions from the doctor, and me explaining what I could remember, the doctor could only assume that my accelerated heart rate from the anxiety had caused me to pass out or black out. When I told him I had a similar attack a few years back, he encouraged me to rest up over the Christmas holidays and to keep well hydrated during the heat. Considering it was just my second attack in a four-year period, there was no cause for alarm.

I got home late that night after catching public transport and a taxi out to my abandoned vehicle. Finally arriving home, exhausted, I drank a couple of glasses of my favourite lime cordial, took some paracetamol and went to bed hoping to sleep it off. Well, that was the plan anyway.

It was dark when I woke up. I don't know what time it was exactly, but I wasn't about to get out of bed just yet. The cordial I drunk had awoken my bladder, so a quick trip to the loo was a necessity.

I stood up from my bed and immediately fell back down. My legs were weak, and I couldn't stand. My head was still throbbing from the cut. As I sat on the bed, I felt my heart rate starting to rise. Surely, I wasn't about to experience a second burst of anxiety in the one day.

Ace of spades, ace of spades, ace of spades. Not me. No. Not this again. I can't deal with this again. I'm too weak to do this a second time. Why are you picking on me? I haven't done anything wrong. I'm a good person. I don't deserve this.

I was drenched from sweat and crawled to the shower. I turned on the cold tap and sat on the shower floor hoping it would cool me down. It wasn't helping. I was burning up. At that moment, I was in complete panic mode.

Ace of spades, ace of spades, ace of spades. Go away. Leave me alone. Are you a demon that wants me? Let me breathe normally please. Stop these horrible feelings. I can't stand it. I can't handle what is happening to me.

I jammed my fingers down my throat and threw up a small amount of black liquid. I managed to get to my feet, marching around the bungalow completely naked and wet. My mind was racing at a million miles an hour.

Ace of spades, ace of spades, ace of spades. How do I make it stop? What am I supposed to do? Please make it stop. Please leave me alone. Get out of my head. Go back to where you came from.

By now I was petrified. I looked for my mobile phone to call the ambulance. I found it and attempted to dial the three simple numbers 0-0-0. I was shaking so badly that I couldn't even hit the first zero before dropping the phone on the ground. The battery fell out and lay next to my phone on the floor. I lined up my phone and booted it hard into the wall, making a hole in the plaster board.

Ace of spades, ace of spades, ace of spades. Fuck off demon! Get the fuck out of my head! Stop trying to hurt me. You can't kill me, I'm too strong, I'm Lee Schraner. I'll fight you to the death. I'm stronger than you think. No fucked-up demon can take me over. I'll beat you. I'm the better man.

I fell to the floor and rolled up into a ball. I was rocking and humming, trying to distract myself from the horrible feelings that had overwhelmed me. I was hitting my head on the floor in a desperate attempt to smash whatever it was, clear out of my skull.

Ace of spades, ace of spades, ace of spades. Bang! Cop that demon. Fucken bang and bang again! I'll smash you out of there. This is my head space. You can try all you like but you will never own me. Fuck off to the land of dickheads and die you slut!

I crawled back into the shower that was still running, trying once again to cool my over-heated body. The freezing cold water hitting my head made it hard for me to hear the awful thoughts. For a few moments, I was able to ignore everything and experience peace. Only when I started to shiver from the water, did I stand up and turn off the tap.

There was blood all over the side and floor of the shower. My head banging must have re-opened the stitched wound, and I was losing a fair amount of blood. I could still feel my heart pounding in my chest, and it wasn't slowing down. Seeing the blood everywhere didn't help calm me down. Maybe I needed to go for a walk. That helped when I was 18, so maybe it would slow my heart rate down now.

Once at the door, I realised I was still naked and couldn't go outside like that. I saw my smashed phone on the ground and a small puddle of blood on the lounge room carpet. I grabbed a shirt off the floor, some undies and shorts, threw on some shoes and approached the front door. I thought I had found a solution to my problem and couldn't wait to start my walk.

I opened the front door, and in an instant, I become fearful of leaving. I didn't want anyone in the outside world to see me like that, even if it was some ungodly hour of darkness. The blood had started to drip on my shirt, so I turned back to the bathroom to get a towel. I saw a face in the mirror that I had never seen before. I saw a pale-white figure, frail, scared and alone. There was blood all over the figure's face, hair messed in every direction, a total stranger to me. The person looked like death, a distant shadow of their past glory.

Ace of spades, ace of spades, ace of spades. Look at you! You look like someone who was smashed up in a fight. Name calling and fighting words can't save you now. You are weak. Take a long, hard look at yourself. You are bleeding, your face is swollen. You have no idea what is going on. The only way you can escape me is to kill yourself. Go on. Do it. You want me gone, then do it. Do it now!

The face was me. I felt weak and helpless. I stumbled into my lounge room, sat in my armchair, and began to cry. Maybe I did have to kill myself to escape the demon. There was something seriously wrong with me. I had to be going crazy. This kind of stuff could not be normal.

Ace of spades, ace of spades, ace of spades. Oh no, here we go again. I'm too weak for this. I have to give in, I can't handle this any longer. Take my arms! Take my legs! Just don't take my mind! Don't send me insane. I have too much to live for.

I swear I felt a rib crack from the pounding of my heart. But I did realise something important while my mind was in outer space. I did have a lot to live for. I was a problem-solver who needed a solution. What could I do to calm myself down and free myself from these morbid thoughts?

Ace of spades, ace of spades, ace of spades. I need to sleep. Sleep will make it go away. I can sleep this off and wake up tomorrow like nothing ever happened.

I was totally white-eyed and wide awake. To sleep now would be a miracle, but I had to try something. It was possibly my only safe way out, so I had to at least give it a go. I put on a DVD that I got for Christmas, lay in bed with my doona up to my neck and was hoping I could doze off with the television going quietly in front of me.

It wasn't working. I jumped out of bed and started striding around in circles. There was no chance I was going to sleep. I had to think quick. I needed to do something to save myself, or I may not make it to sunrise.

By now there was blood on my pillow, bed, lounge room floor and all through the bathroom. I knew I was injured and frail, so I came up with a clever idea. Surely in that state, it wouldn't take much to knock myself out. While knocked out, I would be safe from my mind, allowing my heart rate to return to normal while unconscious. It seemed like a way to keep myself alive.

I stood on the far wall of my room, hunched over, and lined up my door frame.

Ace of spades, ace of spades, ace of spades. Try all you will, you won't escape. I will haunt you forever. There is only one way out and you are too scared to do it. You are a loser!

Off I took. Bang! Take that demon.

Again, I lined up. Fucking bang!

A third time. Bang! I must be close now.

One last time. Big run up.

BOOM!

Lights out.

CHAPTER 22

Diagnosis

Somehow, I woke in the morning alive. I had the worst headache imaginable, which didn't need a bunch of rocket scientists to explain why. I might have had a shocking headache, but I actually felt great. It was good to feel normal again.

My wound had clotted and there was a large chunk of dry blood on my scalp. To try and clean it up, I re-opened the wound and knew I had to go and see a doctor. It was Saturday, but luckily for me, the surgery around the corner was open on a Saturday morning. I had never been there before because I had never been sick. I was about to place my trust and faith in a doctor I didn't even know.

I didn't have an appointment but was hopeful a doctor would see me. When visiting a doctor's office for the first time, you generally get palmed a clipboard full of forms and wait for ages to be seen.

All that jazz was thrown out the window when I walked through the automatic doors.

The receptionist on duty sprung to her feet and ran down the hall, dragging a doctor into the lobby. In a flash, I was sat in a wheelchair and rolled down the hallway to a treatment room. The doctor was asking me about Christmas and the holidays, trying to keep me relaxed and distracted from the needle and thread stitching my head back together.

I must have hit the door frame pretty damn hard, because it took 18 stitches to seal the wound. In all honesty, the pain was nothing compared to my anxiety issues just a few hours before. I felt as though I was sitting in a park, eating baguettes, feeding the ducks, sipping on the best flat-white ever made. I felt at ease and at peace.

Once the emergency procedure was out of the way, I was sat down by the same doctor and put through the questionnaire. He asked me about everything from occupation, to allergies, to medications etc. Then, when that was all out of the way, he finally asked me how I got the head wound.

I sat there in silence for a few moments wondering how the hell I was supposed to tell a new doctor that firstly, I had passed out on the freeway and smacked my head on the ground. Secondly, after it had already been stitched, I smacked my head on the lounge room floor which re-opened the wound. And thirdly, in a fit of panic,

I knocked myself out on a door frame in fear of my life. I mean I walked into this place with a hole in my head and a smile on my face. I had to be crazy.

Without naming the doctor, I can tell you now that he was an expert when it came to mental health. He was willing to sit there, listen to my story and relate to everything I said. He was hesitant at first to prescribe anything, or make a diagnosis for that matter, but he wanted to see me every day until New Years eve to monitor my condition. He even opened the surgery on Sunday to see me the following day as his only patient.

I went home and scrubbed the blood clean from the floor and walls. After a thorough cleaning of the bungalow, I went to the phone shop to buy a new mobile. I then visited the hardware shop to buy some hole-filler, sandpaper, and some white paint. These supplies were all needed to fix the damaged wall. For an office kid, I did a pretty good job on the repair.

To fill the rest of the afternoon, I wanted to go to the bowls club for a roll-up. Being on annual leave during the holidays, I needed to find something to keep me occupied. I didn't want to sit at home bored and give the demonic thoughts an opportunity to return.

I threw my cap on my head and drove around the corner to the club. I had an hour or so on the green with Bundoora legend Mario Cipolla, before packing up and heading home. No one had any idea at that stage of what I'd just been through. I didn't want to admit my sufferings to anyone, not to family, friends, or Bundoora clubmates. As far as I knew, I was going 'mad' and didn't feel it right to communicate that with anybody.

Throughout the week, I saw the doctor every day. There were times of anxiousness at home, but nothing near the level of Boxing Day night. By New Years Eve, I was diagnosed. He told me that I definitely had an anxiety disorder and that based on what I had been through so far, I could expect long bouts of depression to follow. He gave me his personal mobile number as a suicide prevention tactic, demanding I call him any time of the day or night if I ever felt the urge to go through with it.

I didn't touch a drink on New Years Eve, with fear that it may affect my judgement and health. I was in bed before the fireworks went off and spent the evening alone. That night, once again, I was unable to control the onset and severity of my anxiety. I hit my doctor's number on speed dial and told him to come right away.

Within five minutes he was banging on my door. I was in a ball on my lounge room floor, rolling around and humming. I heard the knocks, but I couldn't get up. The door was unlocked, and he let himself in.

My memory of the evening is unclear, other than the fact that I scared the living daylights out of him. In later days, he made it clear to me that he had never seen an attack so severe. He said it was like I 'was possessed by the Devil'. I was so strong apparently, that he couldn't break me out of my body-shaped ball, nor move me into bed. He said my eyes were blank, my face was pale, my humming and gibberish were haunting, and that I seemed to be having an out-of-body experience.

He even mentioned the ace of spades.

I knew that I had found a doctor I could trust. This guy had a sincere care for my health and well-being. I was just a month away from turning 22 and was battling the biggest health scare of my life. He had an honesty about him that gave me comfort. I felt with him in my life, I could begin to fight my mental illness. He saw me daily, free of charge. He probably saved my life.

By mid-January I was given a full diagnosis and placed on antidepressants. I had General Anxiety Disorder (GAD) classed as 'severe', Major Depressive Disorder (MDD) and something called 'psychomotor retardation', a condition that was slowing down my thinking and body movements.

Once diagnosed, I felt it right to tell my parents. Mum had experienced a nervous breakdown when she was young, and I seemed to be following a similar pattern. My parents showed clear concern for my health and wellbeing as expected, and wanted to help in any way they could. I purposely failed to mention Boxing Day and my efforts with the door frame, because I didn't want to scare them. I just told them I was getting treatment from a great doctor, and all was going to be fine.

I returned to work and didn't tell my boss anything about my health. Anything that would potentially cost me my job, would stay private. I was hopeful that on medication and with regular visits to my doctor, that I could beat the illness in the short-term and get on with living a normal life.

What an ignorant boy I was.

CHAPTER 23

Out

I may have played a reserve game or two for Victoria in the past year, but just before turning 22 that January, I was telephoned by Victorian State Coach, Ray Laycock. He had the pleasure of passing on the news that I had made the Victorian Men's side. This call was a total shock to me and completely out of left field. I had no idea I was in the mix to play for the 'Big V' at such a young age, but I took the news with graciousness and appreciation. I was to debut in February, playing second for Mark Jacobsen against New South Wales. The series was being held at Moama.

In my mind, it was the lift I needed to help overcome my mental issues. I now had something exciting to look forward to outside of work and pennant bowls.

My attacks were very frequent, but never once hit me on the bowling green. The green was my element. Nothing in the world could ever distract me from playing a good shot or winning a tough match. Bowls was my escape from reality. It was the place I could go when I wasn't feeling so good.

I debuted for Victoria and really enjoyed the experience. I played terrible, but saying that, I wasn't going to let my performance take precedence over the honour. For all I knew, this could be my first and last series for Victoria, so I was going to make the most of it.

We lost the series 1-2 to New South Wales and our rink also won only one of the three matches. I was convinced that I would be dropped after the series, playing well-under par for that level of competition. I couldn't produce the shots needed on the slick Moama grass greens, feeling well and truly out of my depth. I'd have to wait patiently to see the team for the Alley Shield (National Sides Championship) in Tweed Heads to know my fate.

My time living in Bundoora was over for the time-being, wanting to be closer to work and the city. I wasn't there long until the old couple in the main house decided they wanted their bungalow vacant once again. I got myself an apartment in Carlton to rent, as well as a new car on finance. I thought it was time to forget about the anxiety and start living like a king. So that's what I did.

With my wage increasing regularly, I was spending money as fast as it came in. Between my car repayments, rent, bills, and dining out on Lygon Street every night, I was spending over $1,500 a week.

By the end of February, Bundoora had scraped into the final four of the Premier Division, setting up a knock-out final against Yarraville/Footscray at Glenroy. We wouldn't win the match, but it was a building block for our club after just two years in the competition.

Things continued along normally until the end of March. My health wasn't great by any means, but I chose to ignore it, while living the high life in Carlton. I was as arrogant and cocky as I'd ever been. I was rude, abrupt, and generally not a nice person to be around. This was my inner self acting out, attempting to prove that no mental health concerns could hold me back. In theory, I really thought I was beating them. Once again, I felt 10-foot tall and bulletproof.

It was the calm before the storm.

I never missed a day of work. I was always early, punctual, and reliable. It was the same with bowls. My timekeeping was elite.

On a cool Monday April morning, my alarm for work sounded as usual at 6:30am and it was time to get up for work. But I didn't get up. I never hit the snooze button because I always bounced out of bed looking forward to work. I just rolled over and went back to sleep.

I heard my phone ring here and there, but never answered it. This was totally out of character for me at the time. Normally I was up and about, ready to take on another day.

After what seemed like a short lie in bed, I got up. I needed to ring my boss and make up an excuse for being late. I flicked on the kettle, switched on the television, and got ready for a shower. When I turned the television on, I noticed it was only 8:30am. If I hurried, I could still get to work on time without a need to ring my boss.

I don't exactly remember what the woman said on the television program, but one word echoed in my brain much louder than any other things she said. The word I heard was 'Tuesday'. Initially I thought I must have heard it out of context, so I grabbed my phone to check the time and date.

Bugger me dead, it was 8:33am on Tuesday morning. Out of nowhere, I had slept more than 30 hours! Surely this was a practical joke. Someone had it in for me.

I sat down to think about what I was going to do. How could I explain to my boss that I had been asleep for that long and missed an entire day? I didn't get long to think, because my phone rang, and it was work. I had to answer it.

My boss wasn't upset by any means, more concerned. Not ever missing a day of work, or ever being late for that matter, it was out of character for me. He ordered me straight into work where we could talk privately in his office.

I showered and suited up, arriving at work just after 9:00am. Work was only a ten-minute tram ride from Carlton, and trams went past frequently. I could make up the time swiftly. During that short ride, all I could think about was how I could explain my absence. There was no way around it really. I had to be honest. I had to promise it would never happen again and apologise for any worry or concerns I may have caused.

The meeting was short and sweet. I got on with my work and all was forgiven. I was hoping this would never happen again. Unfortunately, it did. I missed another day the next week and was over an hour late another day.

My boss was a businessman but did have serious concerns for my health and wellbeing. With an 18-month flawless track record and exceptional standard of work, it was obvious to him that something was up.

I decided it was time to come clean and tell him about my mental health problems. He was very understanding, offering to reduce my workdays and hours until I recovered. I'd start having every Tuesday and Thursday off, while working the other three weekdays. I was very grateful for his offer, counting myself lucky to still have a job at all.

The reduced hours had a huge impact on my income. I couldn't afford to eat out anymore and was struggling to meet my rent and car repayments. I had to get better before I went broke. There was no other option.

I hadn't seen my family for a couple of months and Mother's Day was fast approaching. I saw this as a great chance to see the family and make a day of it.

An afternoon at the Melton Country Club, followed by a buffet at the local Chinese Restaurant seemed like a great way to spend a Sunday. I couldn't wait.

We had the best afternoon, and I was really looking forward to a good feed of Asian food. The food was terrific, the drinks great, and the company of family, simply the best.

And then it hit me.

During dinner, I started to cry. I was having such a great day with family that I couldn't understand why my mental health would choose to fail me now. I shot away from the table hoping no-one saw my tears and snuck downstairs to my car. I put the football on to get a live score of the game in Perth. We didn't have smart phones back then, so if you wanted a live score, you had to turn on the radio or television.

I sat in the driver's seat sobbing with the radio on low volume. Within a couple of minutes, Dad opened my passenger side door and sat in the car with me. He closed the door and started talking.

He knew about my mental health diagnosis but had no idea I was struggling that badly. After a few murmurs here and there and a light joke or two, Dad turned deadly serious. He put his hand on my shoulder, looked me straight in the eyes and told me he wasn't getting out of the car until I told him what was really wrong.

Weak, emotional, and tired, I really didn't know what to say. Out of nowhere I just blurted, "I like men!". Just like that, fair dinkum, is exactly how I said it.

Dad took a moment to absorb the news before replying, "Seriously, is that all you had to tell me? What the hell are you crying for? Come back upstairs, wipe your face and we can finish our dinner".

All those damn secretive years bottling my homosexual tendencies in fear, and he gives me an answer like that! I should have bloody well known. My parents were the best parents you could hope for, and yet I kept it secret from them for eight years. Maybe I thought they might be disappointed in me or something. I was their proud son, an academic success, living a life as a professional employee in one of Melbourne's most expensive suburbs. I think it was my shame of who I was that made me keep it secret. I was still coming to terms with it myself in some regard, still going through a period of experimentation and awareness.

I felt an enormous weight lift from my shoulders.

My Dad knew I was gay, and it didn't bother him one bit. If he was hiding any disappointment, he certainly never showed it. Being Maltese, he was family-oriented, and what was said in the car could never take away the love and care he had for me. My only regret was that I never came out earlier.

I told Dad that I would only come back inside on one condition – that he did not tell Mum on Mother's Day. He promised, so I went back upstairs.

Mum called me on my way to work next morning and told me Dad had spoken with her last night. I was fuming because I made him promise not to tell her on Mother's Day. I didn't want her special day remembered for that reason. Mum laughed it off saying that Dad woke her at three minutes past midnight to break the news. He couldn't sleep and had to get it off his chest, and he wouldn't dare break a promise to his eldest son.

Mum told me how much she loved me and that she didn't care if I was gay, a lesbian, or whatever. I was still her baby boy, her first-born, her ray of sunshine. She would love me no matter who I was. In what was a serious conversation, I broke out into laughter. I told her I was glad not to be a lesbian because that would mean I'd still have sex with women, and I didn't want that!

The conversation ended shortly after as I arrived at work. I chose to come out to my workmates that afternoon. Once again, I expected a backlash, or some sickly comments, but I got nothing but support. To me this was a huge moment, but to them, it was a non-event. I couldn't believe that people reacted this way. I was still disgusted at times by my own thoughts and actions, believing everyone would feel the same way. But they didn't.

By the mid 2000's, the world had come a long way. It was socially acceptable in modern Australian society to be a gay man. I felt stupid for not being open with myself earlier.

I could now paint my nails pink, dress up in ladies clothing, flick my wrists, talk with a lisp, be pretentious, and turn my nose up at straight people in a snobby, upper-class, entitled gay way.

I'm only joking. I never did any of those things.

Don't for one minute believe that every gay person acts the same way. Gay men express themselves in many ways and I am overjoyed for all of them. As like a straight male, we are all different. We are individuals. We all live our lives trying to achieve happiness. Your sexual orientation should have no bearing on the way you are treated, spoken to, or seen.

Being gay is a trait you are born with. It becomes part of you, but does not define who you are. If people refuse to accept it, then they have no place in your life. It is their problem, not yours.

It is not a label.

CHAPTER 24

Puff

I made the Victorian team to play the Alley Shield in Tweed Heads. My health was inconsistent, and I continued to sleep very long hours. That particular trip, I was in bed by 7:00pm and sleeping 12 hours a night. My body was mentally and physically exhausted.

My role in Tweed was to lead for the all-conquering Paul 'Pebbles' Dorgan. Recent Australian Singles Champion Bill Cornehls was playing second and the son-of-a-legend, Peter Middleton, was our third.

I tell this story often and it is always a hit.

The very first end of the first match against Tasmania, we left Pebbles five shots down on the head. As we crossed ends, Peter apologised and told our skip that he had two feet for second shot, and we would back him in. Pebbles didn't want a bar of it. He stood in the centre of the green, looked at Peter and said, "I'll clip the front toucher off the jack and then draw the shot".

Chris McKibben, our opposing skip, made it six shots with his first bowl. Pebbles stuck to his guns and drove at the head on his forehand, peeling the closest Tasmanian bowl off the jack and out of play. Chris had plenty of room to add and made it six again. Pebbles switched over to the backhand nonchalantly and drew the shot cold.

My jaw dropped.

As I picked up the mat to roll the jack for the next end, I couldn't help but say out loud "You are God!". It was that moment I realised I was leading for the best player in Australia.

When the Australian side was announced after the series, we all thought Pebbles was guaranteed. His performance across the seven matches was unmatched, clearly the best player at the championships.

The ten names were called out and there was no Pebbles. He was in obvious distress. Australian selection was always subject to conjecture, but even the local club bowler knew he should have made the squad. It was later found out that he wasn't selected because he was 'too fat'. Imagine how that excuse would go down in today's day and age. The world has come a long way in 20 years that's for sure.

On my return to Melbourne, my health deteriorated to a dangerous level. The doctor was totally right. Over the next few months, I slipped into a deep, dark place. I missed so many days of work that I eventually had to be let go. I was so unreliable and unpredictable, my boss had to sever ties with me. It was a cruel blow and left me in financial distress.

My car was repossessed, I was evicted from my Carlton home, I sold everything I had, but couldn't make up the debts I owed. When you are living above your means, a credit card is the norm. For me, it became a massive interest-bearing problem. All up, I was in debt for over $40,000 and was strongly considering Bankruptcy.

I managed to buy an old run-around Ford for $600 and with help from a friend, got the car roadworthy. I visited Centrelink and registered for the dole while hunting for somewhere to live. I used my Carlton address as my place of residence and use to drop by often to check the mailbox for letters.

I was homeless.

I didn't tell a single person about my accommodation issues. I slept in my car, washed in the public toilets in Cameron Park in Bundoora, and parked my car on quiet streets each night. Every now and then I would visit friends and crash on their couch for a night. I did my washing at the coin laundry in Reservoir, aired my car out during the day, and spent a lot of time on the bowling greens.

With very little money on hand, I ate when I could afford to. If invited over somewhere for dinner, I would always go knowing it could be the best thing I ate all week.

I had so much spare time.

By July, the weather was getting really cold, and the car became an ice-box. Most nights were uncomfortable and freezing. I started covering myself in jumpers and jeans and even wore a beanie to sleep. It wasn't perfect, but it did the job.

Next pay day came, and I went to the supermarket as normal. I'd grab some toiletries and snacks. I always had a bag of chips in my car for late night munchies. I had to have some pleasure in my life. I don't know why I bought cigarettes. I had never smoked one in my life, known for my angst against anyone who blew dirty smoke in my face.

I was willing to try anything at that stage to relax. It was probably the most stupid idea I ever had. Cigarettes were expensive, although in comparison, nothing like what they are today. They were around $6.00 a packet at the time for 25's which was a lot of money to me.

To my surprise, they did wonders for me. Not only did they give me warmth, but they also sent me to a relaxed state and made sleeping much more pleasant. But an idea became an addiction. I turned into a chain smoker and used it to relax. I smoked so much that I'd often vomit. Spewing up didn't bother me, if my mind was free from the anxiety.

My appetite was ruined, and I'd go most days without eating any solid food. If I had my smokes on hand, I was happy. If I had to decide between smokes and food with my last few dollars, smokes always won out.

It was very rare for someone to start smoking at 22 years of age. Most addicts start in their early teens and continue it through their lifetime. Nowadays, a lot of people over the age of 50 have found the willpower to give them up, mainly due to ill-health and doctor advice. The health concerns attached to cigarettes meant I should have never considered them as an option. There were other methods of relaxation available at the time. I could have had herbal teas, other medications, vitamins and supplements, and more developed ideas, such as Clinical Psychology.

My problem was that I wanted a quick fix. It seemed to work for me at the time, so I didn't consider anything else. The problem was that by the time I worked out all the other options, and my health began to improve, I was already addicted.

I still smoke today.

CHAPTER 25

Skinny

I withdrew from indoor bowls that winter for two reasons. First, I wasn't well enough to play at the highest level and second, if I made the State team there was no way I could afford the trip away.

By failing to eat regularly, I dropped an enormous amount of weight. At my lightest, I had fallen to 47kg, more than 20kg under my normal weight at the time. Bowls season was just a month away and I had to do something to improve my mental and physical health.

I had to find the inner strength to work again. If I lost my job, I would find another one. I needed a purpose to live and a reason to get up every day. Just one more month of that lifestyle and I would be lucky to be alive. It was a matter of life or death.

After making a few phone calls and attending a couple of interviews, I found a part-time accounting job in the CBD. It was only two days per week, but it was better than nothing. Centrelink would still make me a small payment until I crossed the income threshold, meaning I would have a back-up if I was unable to work.

I found a small bungalow behind a house in Cameron Parade Bundoora for just $100 a week. This was very affordable on my new income, and I planned to be there for at least a year. Almost homeless for three months, I had to get out of my car and into accommodation.

I regret never going to my parents that winter. It is hard to explain why I didn't seek their help or tell them about my troubles. I believe when you are so mentally ill, you think it is your problem and no-one else's. I kept all my problems bottled up inside, believing eventually I could solve them myself. You didn't speak to anyone about your mental health back then, except for your doctor. It was a sign of weakness and insanity. Men had no place publicly to be mentally ill.

Bundoora was entering its third season in premier division. By the start of September, I was still horribly thin. I had begun eating again though, and slowly gaining weight. It was important I played bowls. I disguised my health problems well. Only now and again would someone ask me if I was feeling okay.

Every day I went to work, or bowls was a battle. I would have to pry myself out of bed whether I wanted to get up or not. It's what I had to do to try and get better. I forced myself up, determined to give the day a purpose. I'd go to bed early, sleep more than 12 hours and do it all again the next day. I was trying to fix myself.

We got off to a flyer in premier division and my rink was also going well. By Christmas, we were on top of the ladder and pushing for flag favourites. I won the club singles and the region Champion of Champions singles again. Nick McIntyre and I won the region pairs, and I was through to the final in the newly named 'Under 30 State Singles'.

Christmas, New Years and then my birthday, all came and went. 2005 became the year of getting better, increasing my workload, winning a flag in premier division, and returning to my normal self.

By season close, we finished on top of the ladder and played Darebin City in the double-chance semi-final. We were soundly beaten on all four rinks, and many started to doubt whether we could actually win the gold flag. Melbourne beat Altona in the elimination final and the showdown was set for the preliminary final. We had beaten Melbourne twice that season, but their post-Christmas form was superb. From nowhere, they climbed from the rear end of the ladder, scraped into the final four, and threatened to steal the flag.

I skipped against Russell Green Junior at Glenroy, and our rink match was close all day. Across the board, we remained about 10 shots up overall for a majority of the match, until Melbourne made their move late. With just 15 ends to go, Melbourne hit the front and us Bundoora boys were under enormous pressure.

My next end was as famous as it is infamous. Holding five second shots, I had to take out the Melbourne bowl to score a handful and give Bundoora the lead. The Melbourne bowl was right on the back of the jack, so only a faint edge would dislodge it without moving the jack. I lined up on the forehand as I always did and fired my drive down the green. I looked on the wide side at first, until I realised I was on the wrong bias. My drive missed by a mile, took an edge of an errant Melbourne bowl, ricocheted back, and took the shot bowl out clean as a whistle.

I couldn't apologise enough, but the result stood, and we would claim five shots, going to win the game overall. One of the worst shots I have ever played in my life had given me the luckiest result I have ever had. Call it fate if you will, or just blessed in the moment.

We went on to win the flag 87-85 against Darebin City at Mulgrave Country Club the following Sunday. Nick and I had good rink wins and it made the difference overall. Bundoora had their first ever gold flag, just three years after qualifying for premier division. I broke a jack on a drive that day, with half living at Bundoora Bowling Club, and the other half with me. It still sits proudly in my cabinet.

After pennant, I went on to win the Under 30's State singles final. The State Pairs and Champion of Champions singles was so close yet so far. I gained two silver medals, losing in the finals of both. It would be fourteen years before I'd lose another State final, claiming fifteen gold medals in the same period. Once I reached a final, I would always win it.

During this time, my weight was increasing and my health taking a turn for the good. I felt stronger mentally and physically and as though I was living life again with a purpose. And then, the bowls season was over, and winter arrived.

I had a terrible turn for the worst and once again fell into a dark place. My nervous breakdown had been on and off for eighteen months now and I really wasn't up for the fight again. I lost my job in the city and registered for a Disability Support Pension (DSP) with Centrelink. I was incapacitated to work, and my doctor gave me a six-month medical certificate to ensure I got the government payment.

The pension was enough to pay my rent and bills, but very little was left for food and cigarettes. I slept more hours than I was awake and did nothing but eat, smoke, sleep, and watch television. While I was asleep, I wasn't spending any money, so it was the safest place for me to be. I never had an appetite to eat, but I was determined not to drop my weight to where I was the winter before.

I would visit John 'Macca' McIntyre frequently. He would sit with me, watch television and we'd chat for hours. It was a way for me to fill in the time of being awake, while taking advice on mental health from him. When I was there, I didn't feel alone. Macca suffered from anxiety himself, so he was able to teach me methods of how to deal with it. He gave me some books to read on the subject, which I read each evening before going to sleep.

Much of my focus was on breathing exercises to reduce my heart rate. This step was critical because anxiety attacks would often begin with body tingles and accelerated heart rate. I was experienced in recognising the onset of anxiety, so when I knew it was coming, I'd find a chair, sit down, and start on my breathing exercises.

The one I found most effective was holding my breath for 10 seconds, taking three normal breaths and then repeating. Whether it took five cycles or 50 cycles, I was able to avoid the onset more often than not. The positive results gave me the confidence that I could begin to manage the anxiety in my life. It didn't work every time, but it certainly had positive results.

That winter I visited the bowling club a lot and enjoyed playing the poker machines. I didn't have much money, so I was always on a very small bet. Those evil bandits never paid, but I was able to mix socially with other people that were there. If I needed to get out of the house, and Macca wasn't home, I would go down to the club and play the machines.

As like smoking, I wish I never got addicted. I was a soft and vulnerable target. I was susceptible to addiction and the machines took advantage of me. I would scrounge around for loose change in my car or bowls bag just to get a dollar. It was pathetic. One time I even drove back home to get a dollar coin off my bench that I noticed earlier in the day, only to drive back and lose that single dollar. I was starting to think where I could get more money without a job.

My pension sometimes went just a day or two after I was paid. Once I paid my rent, bought food and smokes for the fortnight, I would blow the rest on gambling. With debt collectors calling daily from my Carlton shortfalls, I began digging myself further into a hole. I wasn't too concerned about my financial position, believing I could sort it out 'later'.

I had an inability to look into the future, focusing on what I had to do to survive each day. I never made plans more than a week in advance, not sure if my health would be well enough to follow them through.

My doctor once again became concerned, believing I was relapsing. I'd hardly been well for a year and a half, but the past couple of months I had made improvements. He knew that despite the medication, specialists, psychology, breathing exercises and anything else I had tried, that my health was still dangerously poor. He was straight-forward and honest with me. He even tried to scare me into a lifestyle change, looking me in the eyes and telling me if I made 30 years of age, it would be a miracle. I knew he was right, but what could I do.

I continued to gamble. The machines preyed on my weakness. Being intelligent, it wasn't like I didn't know they were designed to take my money; it was more of an outlet and distraction for me away from daily life. I saw the expense as a cost of getting better. How naïve. They almost destroyed my life.

I found a way to make extra money on the side. I offered myself online to men for money. My profile online was rude and disgusting, asking for anyone with a big wallet to make contact. I became a slut, seeing multiple men a week. I didn't care who they were, or what they looked like, I just wanted the money to feed my gambling addiction. My visitors included married men and even some lawn bowlers. Whenever I had a burst of anxiety with someone over, I would go to the bathroom and do my breathing exercises. I couldn't let the visitor down, or I wouldn't get paid.

Within a couple of months, I had wiped all my Carlton debt. Through return clientele and growing interest on my online profile, I was booked out for days at a time. I relied on supplements to help me see up to three or four different guys a day. I had never made so much money, and so quickly. I developed a lot of self-hate in that period. I had no appreciation for myself, my body, my mind, and my life. I was only focused on the money. I hated who I was as a human being, with thoughts of self-harm crossing my mind all the time.

I started drinking heavily, coupled with increased smoking and gambling. I never touched drugs. I could have afforded them, but I never tried them. I was taking enough prescription medications at the time for anxiety and depression, that any other drug cocktails could have resulted in an overdose. It was one positive I took out of a disgraceful time in my life. If I was to ever touch drugs, it would have been then. But I never even smoked a joint.

Sitting back today, it is easy to understand that what I did was wrong. It was also illegal. The thought alone of that era makes me feel ill and uncomfortable. I will never provide an excuse for what I did. It happened, and I must live with my actions. I regret it immensely. People make mistakes every day of their lives. I just happened to make a terrible one.

I suffered for that mistake for the rest of my life, completely non-interested in any form of sexual contact. I have little or no libido and live in an asexual companionship. The simple thought of being man-handled is enough to bring back the dark memories. Even being touched on the back or shoulder by a friend, team-mate, or acquaintance, can trigger anxiety and anger. I became protective of my body forever.

I pay for my sins every day.

CHAPTER 26

Bryant

By the end of Spring, I knew things had to change.

I took a night job as a mail sorter for a large company based in Tullamarine. I was employed as a casual but got five shifts a week from Sunday night through to Thursday night. The pay rate was great and surprisingly, I really enjoyed the work.

It would have been easy to sit down, play the victim and be depressed. Instead, I forgot about my university degree and put my focus on being at work every day and doing my job. That I did.

November of 2005, I was invited to Karingal Bowling Club on Melbourne Cup Day by great friend, David Allen. He organised a chance for me to meet my idol, David Bryant. When I had the opportunity to meet the 'Bradman' of bowls, I was never going to let that chance slip.

When I first laid eyes on the great man, I was instantly in awe. My heart began racing and perspiration on my forehead began to appear. I was starstruck.

Despite my nervousness, when shaking his hand, I felt immediately at ease. He introduced himself as 'David' and said that it was his pleasure to meet me. I knew who he was. In that very moment, I understood the meaning of humility. He didn't have an expectation that everyone should automatically know his name. I found that fascinating.

All I could mumble was "I am honoured to meet you Mr Bryant", to which he firmly corrected me on the spot. He was 'David' not 'Mr Bryant'. Again, such humbleness. Should there be anyone in lawn bowls who was addressed in such a way, it should be David.

We must have chatted for about ten minutes, but it seemed more like only a few seconds. It was a privilege to be in the presence of the man, let alone him taking the time to ask about me, my bowling and my life.

Why would David have such an interest in me, when we could talk about his record until the sun went down? The answer was simple. He was a down-to-earth gentleman who took a genuine interest in everyone he spoke to. He didn't have to try to be friendly or kind, it was simply in his nature. It was then I realised I had chosen the right idol in our sport.

David was in Australia for the 25th Anniversary Singles event against our own homegrown hero, John Snell. Two years before I was born, Bryant and Snell played an epic World Singles final at the City of Frankston Bowling Club in early February 1980. This upcoming three-match series was designed to celebrate that great match – and who could resist watching Bryant and Snell go at it three more times in their multiple-decade rivalry.

Both John and David were about to have a training session in preparation for the event when David politely asked to join some of the local club members for a game of fours. No-one was going to say no to David, but he did state he would only play on one condition. He pointed at me and said, "I will play fours if I can lead for this young man".

Here I was at a club I had never been to, joining some locals for a roll-up and having David Bryant lead for me. The day could not possibly get any better, surely. Well, it did.

Without a roll-up, David placed the mat, rolled the jack, and drew two touchers with his first two bowls. Just watching him in his unique style, his pipe now long gone, I couldn't help but smile from ear-to-ear.

Not only did he put on a leading clinic in our ten-end match, but David also picked up bowls, patted his team mates on the back and encouraged every shot they played. It was just the same as if he were playing for a World gold medal. That's probably what struck me the most. It was the competitiveness that drove him. He wanted to win every game he played.

Despite being a close match, we snuck in. He shook everybody's hand, kindly telling them all "well-played".

As we were packing our bowls away, David tapped me politely on the shoulder and asked if he could show me something.

He walked over to the bank and lifted a boundary peg from its home. He handed it to me with an internal smile and said, "shoot me as if this boundary peg was a rifle".

I didn't want to shoot him.

After being asked a second time, I braced, held the boundary peg like a rifle and lined up to shoot him. "Voila!" he said with a huge grin on his face, "if that is the perfect point of balance to shoot a rifle, then it must also be the perfect point of balance to deliver a bowl". Confused, I looked down at my feet. My pivot foot was turned and my front foot pointing at him, my target.

I was speechless. I just had a two-minute coaching lesson with David, and it would change my bowling life forever. What an epiphany. From that day forward, I delivered the bowl in that stance.

David was the epitome of everything I wanted to be in our sport. I wanted to be a winner, a gentleman, a legend! His aura made me jealous. It made me want to be a better bowler, but most importantly, it made me want to be a better human being.

My severe anxiety and overwhelming depression had been controlling my life for the past two years. I thank David for being part of my recovery. His lust for life and love for lawn bowls inspired me to work on the long road to recovery. He made me feel like life was worth fighting for. He was right.

The day we lost him was just one week before the release of my book, 'In the Zone II – Secrets of a World Champ'. I felt that the least I could do, was to dedicate my book to him.

He simply was the greatest bowler to ever play our sport. He was the most humble, graceful, friendly, sportsmanlike, and skilled player we have ever witnessed. The bowls world lost an irreplaceable master when he passed away.

Without a doubt in my mind, there was and only ever will be, one David Bryant.

The summer went by fast. Bundoora missed the finals by a single point and our flag defence was not to be. My team of four won the rink premiership, but it wasn't enough to get us into the final four.

In early March, Bundoora was invited to Darebin City to take on the Australian Commonwealth Games Men's team. Darebin City was only a 15-minute drive from Bundoora and the squad was seeking all the match practice they could get before the Melbourne Commonwealth Games.

We picked the best five players we had and agreed to the practice match. I skipped pairs with Mario Cipolla, and we managed to beat Barrie Lester and Nathan Rice in straight sets. I then played singles against Kelvin Kerkow and again, won in straight sets. It was no secret that over the past couple of years I had worked hard on slow grass greens, and this paid dividends that day. The triples might have lost, but Bundoora won the contest two rubbers to one. It was an honour and a thrill to play against the Australian Men, who would go on to win Singles gold, Pairs bronze and Triples gold.

At work, I began to feel normal again. I was always on time, doing a solid job and scoring the maximum five shifts per week, every week. Even though I continued to skip in premier division and play for Victoria, I wasn't treating bowls as important. It was more about getting my whole life back on track through work.

The winter was all about work. I had stopped playing indoor biased bowls after failing to be selected for Australia at the trials, seeing the sport as a distraction rather than a future. It was a brave decision as I had been very successful in the sport, but it had to be done. To start work on time, there was no way I could play pennant or night competitions beforehand.

I was selected for Australia at Under 25 level to take on New Zealand. I skipped the fours and triples, helping score a 3-0 victory on foreign soil. It was my first time in green and gold and I loved it. It opened the door ever so slightly to the Australian Men's team. Maybe it was the two wins against the Aussie side that March that got me in the spotlight. Even though I had been playing State bowls for two years, I was relatively unknown. Right place, right time maybe?

I had a health turn early that summer, failing to attend work for the first time. Actually, let me re-phrase that. I drove to work ready for my shift and fell asleep in my car in the car park. When I woke, it was daylight, so I knew I had missed my shift. I'd later be dealt the ultimate punishment even after 15 months with a flawless record. I was sacked.

Luckily for me I had saved enough money to get through the season, coupled with the Disability Pension I was to receive again on an extended medical certificate.

My sixth and final season at Bundoora was successful in an individual capacity, but well below par as a pennant side. We finished 8th, just a rink clear of relegation after losing Adam, Luke, Nick, Brent, and others. I only stayed there an extra year because of my cheap rent of $100 a week. Relying on saved funds and a pension, my bank account was bone dry by the season end and I felt it was time to move on. Again, my four would win the rink premiership. It helped the side survive in Premier Division, but ultimately, we were clutching at straws to be competitive.

After turning 25, I won the State Pairs with Mario Cipolla, the club singles, and the State Under 30 singles, for the third time. I also teamed up with Joel Simmonds and Paul Dorgan to win the triples gold medal at the Moama Grand Prix event, getting past Kelvin Kerkow, Mark Casey, and Bill Cornehls in a thrilling tie-break final.

I attended a coaching interview at Karingal Bowling Club that Winter, recommended by David Allen. After facing the Board of Directors and fierce negotiations, I scored a two-year deal. My time at Bundoora would come to an end in the winter of 2007, making Karingal my new home.

Frankston here we come.

CHAPTER 27

Franga

Subject to popular belief, I found Frankston to be the best place I ever lived in Victoria. A two-bedroom apartment on the shore of the beach, cost me just $150 per week. I had two major shopping centres, a nightlife, and even a police station across the road.

That spring, at 25, I was lucky enough to be selected again to represent Australia against New Zealand. This time I skipped triples and played singles. Again, we would beat them 3-0 on their own home greens. I won all my singles matches and had two wins and a draw in the triples. It was an Australian demolition of the young Kiwis, hardly losing a match over the three-day event.

Karingal was a very strong club in the region but had two major problems. In the club's history, they had never won a Nepean premier division flag, and it was 37 years since they had won a division one flag. The ladies were very successful and had won multiple top-grade pennants. My two-year deal had to secure the top two Saturday flags, or I would be seen as a failure.

I spent a lot of time around the club. Still on the pension, my part-time coaching contract earnt me enough income to avoid full-time work. My official role asked for six hours per week, but I always did at least double that. I took pride in my coaching and worked very hard with bowlers of all levels.

Karingal had two grass greens at the time, with both always running a second or two below the competition average. To me, the slow greens provided an avenue to success. The premier side were taught from day one to play ditch-to-ditch. The lead players were drilled into long jack rolling and reaching with every first bowl. The seconds were encouraged to develop their driving skills for aggression on shorter ends, and to play all their draw shots on longer ends between the jack and the ditch. Thirds were taught to play a more active role and take responsibility as a vice-skip. Their relationship with the skip would be crucial to success. Skips were taught game plans around full-length ends, mats up the green, and a draw/drive approach. This level of bowls was reasonably high, but minimal weight conversion shots had a low level of success and had to be eliminated.

The club bowlers and Board of Management were very supportive of me in my first season. They always kept a close eye on my coaching to ensure their investment was worthwhile.

I won the club singles as expected and went on to win the region Champion of Champions singles. I also won the association fours, but we were beaten in the regional final. Mario Cipolla and I received direct entry into the Australian Open Pairs for our State championship winning effort and would make it all the way to the final. In a close contest, we went down in a tiebreaker to Gary Lawson and Ryan Bester, grateful for our Australian silver medal.

The premier division side was incredible. We adopted the war cry 'Vincero!' from Puccini's Turandot, made very famous by Pavarotti in the ballad 'Nessun Dorma'. Simply translated, it means 'I will win!'. Every time someone played a great shot in pennant, they were encouraged to call 'Vincero!'.

We won every game in the home and away season and entered the double-chance semi final full of confidence. The Nepean Association showed a huge lack of wisdom when selecting Somerville as the venue to play Hastings. Somerville was an artificial carpet green, and Hastings also played on a carpet surface. It was a disadvantage to us and was always going to be a challenge. To make matters worse, Somerville had many teams participating in finals, so the biased 'blazers' (the name I gave administration officials), appointed a Hastings bowling member as umpire for the match.

The match was very close all the way and full of intensity. It will be remembered for two reasons, both of which became very infamous.

One of the players in my rink completely lost his cool and made a personal verbal attack on a Hastings player in a wheelchair. It was an horrendous few moments and I had absolutely no idea what to do. My coaching limits were being tested and I had to do something. For the game to progress, and not be abandoned, I had to calm my player down and get his focus back on the bowls. I already knew that he was guaranteed to be suspended and miss the rest of the year at least, but I had to keep that to myself.

The second infamous incident was between the biased Hastings umpire and me. I hit a head late in the game when we were in trouble. When the dust settled, we held six shots. There was about two metres for my opposing skip to draw the shot with his last bowl, even though the jack sat just inside the rink boundary line. The Somerville green was unpredictable in the wind, especially on the narrower hand, and my opposing skip had to draw on that side. When he let his bowl go, the wind came right up, and the bowl refused to turn at all. I think it went more out than in.

When it stopped, it fell against the normal bias of the bowl and outside the boundary line. My third called out 'six shots Karingal' and I was thrilled. That was until the opposing third called the umpire to use the mirror on the bowl that was clearly out.

Picture this – Karingal 88, Hastings 87, with six ends to go overall. A count of six would put us seven up with five ends to play and a spot in the grand final would surely be ours.

I have never cheated in bowls. 99.9% of the bowlers who have ever played the sport are clean, honest, and respectful of fair play. If this bowl wasn't at least a full bowl outside of the boundary line, I'll go eat my hat. I even joked with the umpire that he would need a banana-shaped telescope to call that bowl in.

He deliberated longer than I thought, but I wasn't concerned. My opposition skip had his hands on his head, while my leader had picked up the mat ready for the next end. Even the naked eye could see the bowl was so far out of bounds, that the umpire call was unnecessary.

When the umpire called the bowl 'in bounds' I lost my cool. I asked him to do it again as he had clearly made a mistake, to which he replied, "No, my call is final".

Regrettably, I gave him a verbal barrage, labelling him a 'cheat' amongst other things. I had steam coming from my ears as their leader rolled the jack for the next end.

We lost the match by two shots. Our team manager made an official complaint about the umpiring call to the 'blazers', but it was dismissed. Their reasoning was understandable, saying that the umpire's call is final whether correct or not.

To my dismay, I received an official letter of complaint from the umpire and the Hastings Bowling Club that week, about my reaction to his umpiring call. My other teammate had been justifiably suspended for six months, but now they were trying to suspend me too. A cheating club and umpire had the nerve to put me at blame for the situation, even though in my opinion, they had placed the sport in disrepute.

After direct consultation with officials at Bowls Victoria, I was advised to send a letter of apology to the umpire and club. They were positive that if I apologised and regretted my actions, that the club would drop the official complaint. I bit the bullet and put my club first. They needed me to play the semi-final the next weekend, so I had to write the letter.

I faxed a letter of apology to Hastings Bowling Club, addressed to the umpire and the club itself.

That Friday, Hastings contacted Bowls Victoria saying that my two-page apology letter had only come through as one page. It took them three days to tell Bowls Victoria this. They didn't even contact me in the interim, to re-fax the letter. From our end, the fax had gone through as two pages successfully. It was a conniving delay tactic.

They conveyed to Bowls Victoria that my apparent incomplete apology letter was not accepted and that they wished to pursue my potential suspension. By this stage I was extremely worried. Karingal had to play their nemesis Somerville at Long Island in the preliminary final the next day, and I wasn't cleared to play.

The delay tactic was their downfall. Bowls Victoria could not hold a hearing at such short notice, and it was set for the following week. I was free to play.

We beat Somerville comfortably that Saturday and lined up a re-match with Hastings in the grand final. The venue was Long Island, thankfully on grass, set for the following Sunday so all other divisions and spectators could watch. My focus now was on beating the complaint.

I told Bowls Victoria that I was willing to sign a Statutory Declaration about the cheating umpire and was even willing to go to court if they suspended me. Karingal were willing to pay my costs. I also conveyed that my actions toward the umpire were not acceptable, and that in the heat of the moment I lost my cool. I couldn't believe that I had been cheated out of a match – Bowls Victoria believed me.

I had a flawless record. I was a Victorian State representative, a multiple State champion and always respected the sport of bowls. I refused to stand down.

By Thursday, Bowls Victoria notified Karingal that the complaint from Hastings had been dropped. Whether it was the threat of court action or fear of being labelled 'cheats' in the public eye, the club in their one moment of wisdom, dropped their complaint. Now, I was on a mission to put them to bed once and for all.

Sunday was predicted to be 40 degrees, so the Grand Final was scheduled for a 9:00am start to avoid the heat. This was great for Karingal. The earlier the start, the slower the green. We knew we had them covered on a slow grass surface.

Every player was at Karingal no later than 8:00am that morning, rolling up before the big match. Our green was pushing 12 seconds at that time of day, so we were anticipating Long Island to be 13 or 14 seconds at best.

When arriving at Long Island at 8:30am, we walked from the car park to their single green. We couldn't help but notice the sprinklers going full pelt, with some surface water visible on the green. A young guy in a fluro shirt ran over to the tap and turned off the water. The blazers had failed to notify Long Island about the early grand final start due to the heat, and the greenkeeper was simply getting water on the surface to ensure it didn't burn in the afternoon under a hot Frankston sun.

All our side smiled like Cheshire cats. Our ear-to-ear grins knew that a damp, slow green, would give Hastings no chance against us. The stars were aligning. We had to win the match for our club. We had to win the match for our legend clubmen and mates, Ted Connors and Max Simpson, who had died during the season. The Karingal Kangaroos were about to turn on one of the great grand final performances. We had worked harder than anyone else, trained better than anyone else, and won more games than anyone else. It was our time.

When the cards were drawn, I was pitted to skip against the Hastings Club President, who so desperately tried to get me suspended. I was pumped – and I mean pumped!

In our team huddle, I gave a passionate and emotional speech about what lay in front of us. I demanded that we be loud, show no respect to our opposition, and to make sure we did everything we could to win the premiership. I pointed fingers at individuals and fired them up. I yelled in the faces of players I knew would react. I could see spots of saliva flying from my mouth as I widened my eyes and challenged the side to make it the most important match of their lives. I swore and I stomped. I have never made a speech like that ever before and, would never do again. This match was about ownership and revenge. It was about sending our opposition home red-faced with their tails between their legs. There was to be no friends made on the green that day, not with a club who had cheated their way into a grand final.

The roll up began, and man-o-man was the green heavy! It was lucky to be 11 seconds. The flag was going to be ours.

Geoff Watt and his team scored six shots on the first end, on a long end. Hastings couldn't get their bowls up to the head. Phil Ashman and his team got off to a flyer, winning the first 11 ends of their match. It was the best game I had ever seen Phil play.

He was untouchable. Grant Burley skipped our third rink, and he was down, but we had his margin well and truly covered. They just needed to stay close and the other three rinks would get us home. My rink started well and at half time, we led 17-4 after 13 of the 25 ends.

Overall, we had Hastings 61-28, with Phil 19-0 on 11 ends against Duncan Parkinson. Every time he played a great shot he would run down the green yelling, "It's just like ordering pizza. Simple. One with the lot mate!".

The second half was party time. Even when Burley finished his rink with a 14-37 scoreline, we still led by 23 overall with only 10 ends to go. Hastings had started to hit back as the green quickened, so we had to make sure we held on.

I was one down on my head with one second shot. After a closer look, I could see both of their bowls lined up to go out of the head, leaving us with a count of five. It would be match over if I got it.

I lined up on my forehand, fired down my blue rock, and I knew it was good. I screamed at the top of my voice, "It's an exhibition boys!" and got down on one knee to salute the crowd. Both Hastings bowls disappeared as my rink jumped up and down. We got the five shots and surely the game was over.

The final 20 minutes of the grand final saw Hastings try their darndest, but to no avail. At 34 shots up with just four ends to go, the maths were in our favour and it was time to call the game.

Karingal Bowling Club had finally taken that elusive step and won the top-grade flag. My coaching contract was sure to continue for many years to come. Our hard work and long end tactics had paid off. We were by far the best team in the competition and deserved it.

Our only sadness of the day was the tears for our suspended player. He was so happy that we won it, but obviously distraught he wasn't a part of it.

The final score was 116-82. My rink won 37-6 in a fiery performance, giving our opposition nothing. My disrespectful attitude towards Hastings was clear for all to see, and even today, I don't regret it one bit. They were the ones who put me in the mood for blood. I wanted revenge, even if it was the last thing I ever did. I wanted to make sure they would think about that day for the rest of their lives. I wanted them to feel the pain. I wanted them to suffer.

If you poke the bear, you get scratched.

I couldn't help but include a poem of the victory written by one of our premiership players, Ken Ridout. Please enjoy it as I still do today. We did it for Max and Ted!

Thank you, Ken, for giving me a memory to last forever.

VINCERO!
It was grand final day at Long Island,
It was a sight you'd never seen.
For a bowling mob from Karingal,
Had taken over their sacred green.

The team was all primed up,
Lee had said his pre-match say.
We were ready for this occasion,
Our team had come to play.

The red and white crowd sat,
They were full of apprehension.
They bought fold up chairs and sandwiches,
With coffee to ease the tension.

The knockers showed their faces,
You know, the ones who hope you fail.
Well, we were going fix them up,
With the swish of a Kanga's tail.

The green was timed as normal,
They said it was fourteen.
We knew it wouldn't be that quick,
Maybe they'd had a dream.

Doggie began with a six at the start,
Are we going to win?
Mate we're going to blow 'em apart,
I think we'll shit it in!

Phil was on fire all day,
Eleven ends on the trot.
It was just like ordering pizza mate,
A large one with the lot!

At eleven forty-five we ate,
And enjoyed a cup of tea.
A half had gone already,
We led by thirty-three.

Hastings came back firing,
Like we knew they would.
We beat them in every way,
Just like a good team should.

Grant's rink had to fight,
Their backs were to the wall.
They won four of the last five ends,
Contributing to the overall.

Lee was on a mission,
As he launched a stunning drive.
He screamed, "It's an exhibition!"
As he picked up a match-sealing five.

The monkey was off our backs,
It had finally sunk in.
Karingal had won the Nepean flag,
What a magnificent win!

I heard angels calling from above,
Our war cry we well know.
I think it was Max and Ted.....
They were singing, "Vincero!"

CHAPTER 28

Glory

After winning the premiership, my focus immediately turned to the Victorian Champion of Champions singles at Swan Hill. I was in good form and expected to play well. I truly believed it was my turn to win it.

The drive from Frankston to Swan Hill was epic. My coaching funds had dried up and I was getting by on my pension. The cheapest motel I could find was $140, so I decided to pack a doona and pillow and sleep the night on the back seat of my car.

By morning I was stiff and sore from the awkward sleep. I regretted not paying for the motel room. I struggled through my round of 16 match against Wally Dunstan, dropping four shots on the first end. After an intense battle, I snuck home 25-22 in a thriller, setting up a quarter final match with one of Victoria's greatest ever players, Wayne Roberts. This match would start an awesome rivalry that would continue for years to come. We were both good friends, Hawthorn supporters in the AFL, and respected each other as people and bowlers. It was always going to be a cracker.

Down 22-23, I scored three shots to sneak through in my second thriller of the day. I was backing myself on full length ends when the match got tight. I wasn't hitting any drives, so mat control was crucial.

The following day I won my semi final 25-20 against local, Peter Arthur. I was in big trouble early in that match, down 6-13 and lying three down on the head, before a thunderbolt drive sunk the jack for three shots to start my comeback. I remember being so determined to win the match, shouting "I'm not done with yet!" when I hit that drive. It was probably the first drive I hit for the event. I didn't miss again after that.

I played Bendigo young gun, Brad Holland in the State final. After three long matches, I was struggling physically. Behind at 17-20, I got a serious case of cramping. I looked like a goner at that stage, continually apologising to Brad for cramp delays. I couldn't put a bowl down without my left hamstring grabbing. I had to stretch on the bank before every bowl, hoping it would hold until I let the bowl go. My slow and deliberate action was crucial on this silky-smooth fast surface.

I scored seven consecutive shots to go ahead 24-20, then dropped a single. The next end I held the match. Brad played a great shot, trailing the jack off my close bowl, sitting just under three feet away from the jack. To me, this was match point number one. Could I take it?

I stuck to my own tactic of drawing across the line and ignored the open hand draw for fear of tracking down fresh, untouched grass. My backhand draw felt like good weight, but it appeared a touch wide. About five metres out, I knew it was lineball. I was yelling, "Drop! Drop!" encouraging the bowl to turn under the short stuff. It listened, turning in for the match winning bowl.

I had the mat in my hand and my initial reaction was to throw it metres in the air. I was ecstatic. That mat launching celebration became a trademark of mine in later years when I won a major event or title. The crowd had erupted, on their feet, clapping the two players from the green. It was handshakes all round and in for a nice cold beer.

Robert Middleton presented me with the medallion and winner's cheque. It was very special for me to have him there. He was a legend of Victorian bowls and was also the marker when I first won the Victorian Under 25 singles against Barrie Lester some years before. This was the happiest I had been in some time, feeling free for just a moment or two from my mental demons.

That win would be my first of eight State Champion of Champions singles in the next 16 years, across three different States. It became my pet event and one I always felt privileged to play in.

Winter came and I felt well enough to return to work. I had gained some weight and was as healthy as I had been in a long time. I scored a job as a Tax Accountant in Highett and even bought myself a 5-series BMW on finance. My credit wasn't great, so the interest payments were high, but with the income I was earning from work and bowls coaching, it was very affordable.

The next season at Karingal was devoted to defending the premiership. We won 17 of our 18 matches and finished clear on top of the ladder. During preparation for the finals, I received notice from the Board of Management at the club that after the season, my coaching services were no longer required. I was shattered. I loved the club and where I was living. It was a disappointing decision by the club to say the least. They insisted that I had done what they wanted me to do, and investing in my coaching any further would be a waste of money.

The news leaked through the club via gossip, and some players in the premier side got the news. It totally deflated them. They knew I wasn't going to be at Karingal the following year and it affected their performance. In a shock result, we were smashed by Somerville in the double-chance semi final at City of Frankston by a whopping 51 shots. My rink scraped in by a single, but it was nowhere near enough to cover the other rink defeats.

The preliminary final was against Dromana at Rosebud and despite a more concerted effort, the team went down by two shots overall. What made the game more disappointing was that I had won my own rink 36-12 and still, it wasn't enough to get us over the line. The timing of the club's decision had broken the heart of our players, and I wasn't able to lift them for the finals. It was a disaster to go out in straight sets, unable to defend out title. I was so devastated by the whole situation that I began looking for a new bowling club There was no coming back from that.

The season for me personally was beyond belief. I won every single pennant rink I skipped, and my run in the Association and Region events would break a record. I won every event; the association singles, pairs, triples, fours, and champion of champions singles, with a 25-0 scoreline against John Daniel from Long Island in the final, in just 10 ends. I went on to win all events at region level except the State singles, beaten by Eric Sellenger from Dromana. I was so close to the perfect personal year.

The very week I lost that singles match, I received notification that I had made the Men's Australian Squad. I couldn't believe it. Here I was playing as good as I ever had, and I was rewarded with one of just ten spots in the Australian squad. I had played the two previous years in the Under 25 Australian team, but this honour was just so much more prestigious. All I had to do was keep doing what I was doing and surely, I would score an Australian cap sooner rather than later.

I was invited to attend the Asia Pacific Games trials in Kuala Lumpur. This unfortunately clashed with the State pairs and State triples finals, so I had to get substitutes. Thank goodness Bowls Victoria now has a Champion's week, avoiding clashes with Australian squad member duties and responsibilities.

I felt as though I performed decently on the super-heavy Malaysian greens. The two years at Karingal had made heavy greens my new comfort zone, and I was able to play to a high standard. I led a handful of games in pairs for Mark Jacobsen and Leif Selby, losing just one match against the Malaysians. I thought I was a genuine chance to make the five-man Asia Pacific team.

A second trial was set a month away at Soldiers Point, where the team would be named for the games. I remained confident in the coach's adage that 'horses will be picked for courses', believing I was a genuine chance for the team.

When arriving back from Malaysia to Melbourne, I was severely under the weather. I was so sick from the 'Malaysian Malay' that I couldn't keep any food down at all. I was drinking a heap of fluids to try and keep hydrated, but I was in all sorts of heck. The State Champion of Champions singles finals were just a day away at Altona and I was worried about putting up a solid defence.

Against Bob Darby from Edithvale, I put up a decent effort to win 25-17 in the round of 16 match. In the quarter final, I played Darren Yates from Darebin City. By this stage of the day, I was violently ill.

I warned Darren before the game that I would have to make many runs to the toilet and apologised to him in advance. I was spewing up, had violent diarrhoea, and a pounding headache. I was weak, malnourished, and found it difficult to concentrate.

Just three ends in, I was 0-8 down and I knew my fate was set. I didn't have the strength to fight on and I knew I was going to lose.

I don't know how the match turned around from memory, because I can barely remember anything of it. Winning 25-18 from where I was and how I was feeling, was nothing short of a miracle. It had to be one of the toughest experiences I had ever dealt with on a bowling green. I was so exhausted that I couldn't even drive home. I had a friend with me, who was able to do the trip back to Frankston.

Before getting home, we stopped at Frankston Hospital. I had a couple of fluid bags put through me, drunk Lucozade, and took some gastro-stop tablets. When sent home, I did what I was told and got immediate rest.

I woke up right as rain the next day. I grabbed my bottles of Lucozade and my gastro-stop tablets and jumped in the car for bowls. Back to Altona I went.

I turned on a great semi-final, beating Michael Vesikko from Sunbury 25-18 in a high-quality match. I met David Shaw from Brighton in the final and had the opportunity to claim the title back-to-back. It had been 51 years since a Victorian had defended their Champion of Champions singles crown. Of course, it was none other than Legendary Hall of Famer, Glyn Bosisto, who all up won seven State Champion of Champions singles titles.

The final was a non-event as I coasted to a 25-11 victory, etching my name in Victorian lawn bowls history. The mat was launched once again into the heavens.

Now I was chasing Bosisto.

CHAPTER 29

Brighton

I lost my job in Highett due to too much time off. Through the odd days of mental health struggles and the new bowling commitments, I didn't have the strength to do it all. Once again, I would be back on the pension.

The second trial for the Asia Pacific games was another successful effort. I was pleased with my play and quietly confident of making the cut. My interview at the end of the trials before the team was announced was uncomfortable and disappointing. In fact, I found it downright personal. The selectors and coaches had left me out of the team for the games.

Somehow the hierarchy had found out I was homeless for a period and living out of my car. They also knew of my long battle with anxiety and depression, and that I was on a disability pension. They were aware that I was unemployed, and this made me unreliable.

It was even apparent that some teammates refused to room with me, whether it be about my sexuality, or for other reasons. Those players had conveyed that message direct to the coaches. The explanation was never given to me as to why I missed the team, but I knew deep down it wasn't to do with my bowls. These issues would have never been brought up in that interview if they weren't part of my non-selection, so I was adamant they were the main causes.

I thought I had been brought into the team specifically for that event. My skillset was now slow grass greens, and I was a good player on them. Obviously, I had been misled. I honestly felt like I was just making up the numbers and purely brought into the squad to give their selected team competition on slow tracks.

I was shattered that I missed the team, but angrier about the whole process. I thought the entire situation was unsatisfactory at the time, but I kept my mouth shut. I believed deep down that I had been discriminated against, but who was I to judge. I was new to the team and had to 'fit in', to be a part of it. It crossed my mind to exit the environment prematurely, believing it was toxic and likely to affect my mental health. But I held off, trying to be positive about the opportunity of playing for Australia, and the work I had done to make the initial squad.

Looking for a job and a new bowling club, I met with Geoff Maskell and Ken Armstrong from Brighton. A club management position had come up in line with the brand-new facility being built in Dendy Park. The position would provide me with a full-time income as well as all the time off for bowls I needed. How could I refuse?

The trip from Frankston to Brighton in the mornings was a nightmare. It was close to an hour and a half through peak hour traffic and up to two hours in the rain. It meant I had to be up bright and early every day to make sure I was at work by 9:00am. Copping the peak traffic on the way home too, I never really sat down for dinner until after 7:00pm. The days were long and they were taking their toll.

We were a division one side with aspirations of being promoted to premier division. We were drawn in a tough section though, with recently relegated Bundoora and a strong Lalor outfit, the biggest threats.

Brighton knew nothing of my poor health history, so I saw it as a chance to start on a clean slate and become a responsible worker once again. I worked hard, but also took plenty of breaks during the day. My office was right near the main entrance, so I could always sneak out for a smoke and still hear the phone if it rang.

Pennant arrived and the blue indoor green was christened with a thrilling one-shot win over Lalor. The indoor green was such an advantage that our first win started a run of 26 more straight wins over three and a half years, before we eventually lost on it for the first time.

I won the club singles by beating Geoff in the final and kept the door open for a hat-trick of State Champion of Champions singles titles. My 42-game winning streak came to an end in the Region final when I blew a 15-1 lead against Ted Russell from Elsternwick Club to lose. What a bummer!

We won 16 of our 18 pennant matches that year but finished third behind Lalor and Bundoora. The three teams were such a standout in the section, that not one of the other seven sides even got close. We would all win 16 games, with only rink points separating us in the end. Bundoora beat us comfortably in the first final on their home deck and we were eliminated from the competition.

I entered the QLD Open at Bribie Island, pairing up with Neville Rodda. I also played triples with Todd Simmons and 14-year-old Dylan Fisher, as well as entering the singles. Despite being knocked out in the final eight of the pairs and singles, Todd, Dylan, and I, would go on to claim the Gold Medal in the triples.

I scored an invitation to the Golden Nugget Prestige Singles and did well enough to make the final. Steve Glasson was too good for me in the big dance, cleaning me up 25-15 and I had to be satisfied with second place. It was 20 years since a Victorian had made the final, so it was pleasing to at least be noticed. Second place in that extraordinary field is nothing to be ashamed of.

It was a great first year at Brighton, with my bowls and health all appearing to be going well. I was doing a good job at work and spending extra hours helping the club get off the ground in its new location. I was still in the Australian squad and knew the next year or so would be crucial to get that elusive green and gold cap. I had to do something special to make a mark on the sport. I wasn't about to die wondering.

I moved to Bentleigh to be closer to work. It saved a lot of travel time, so I could use that extra time to train hard on the greens. As the season approached, I found myself working upward of 60 hours per week. Sometimes I would open the club café at 7:00am to serve the soccer players their breakfast and coffees, and then close the bar at midnight after a function. It was no wonder I burnt out and my mental health deteriorated dramatically.

I had some deep and meaningful meetings with Board Members, eventually coming clean about my history of poor mental health. Ken was nothing but a gentleman to me through the whole ordeal. He genuinely understood what I was going through, and as Chairman, he would support me in any way he could. If only Ken had the support of other Board Members, I would be safe in my role. Unfortunately, in the world of running a business, other members of the board could only see it in black and white – I was either there or I wasn't. I even overheard gossip amongst members that my position was under threat, and this didn't help my mental state.

The stress of losing my job there only made matters worse. I was having exhausting daily bursts of anxiety and sleeping many hours through the depression. I hung onto my job into the summer, but only just.

Pennant was under way by October, and we started the season a few cattle light from the previous year. Our side was obviously weaker, but it didn't hamper our determination to be successful.

By November we had won five of our six matches and were going well. My own personal form was well down due to ill health and the thoughts of losing my job. To relieve that angst, I did the creditable thing and submitted my notice of resignation. I was leaving the role, but not the club. I stayed because of the support shown by Ken and Geoff and their willingness to help me through the mental pain and anguish.

For what was about the fifth time I could remember, I again sort an extended medical certificate and found myself back on the disability pension once more.

The Australian Squad changed coaches, so I was excited about the prospects of a new culture. Trials for the 2010 Delhi Commonwealth Games had started, and I was going to give it everything I had to make it. I wasn't working, so I had all the time I needed to rest, sleep, and then hit the greens to train hard.

We had a camp in Cairns on an artificial green, in unbearable hot and humid conditions. With Delhi offering artificial greens for the games, it was all about trialling on carpet greens in the weather extremities that would likely exist over in India. Things were getting fair dinkum for selection and many of the squad members were friendly on the outside but determined as hell on the inside. Commonwealth Games only come around every four years, so this was a major period for any aspiring Australian bowler.

Our next camp was at Mona Vale, where head coach Rex Johnston had us playing all different formats and positions against each other. There was hardly any skills training or drills by this stage, as it was assumed every player had done their work and had come prepared. It was all about what combinations could prove successful against other selected teams.

At the conclusion of the Mona Vale camp, the side was selected to play a warm-up series against England at Moama. It was a one-off series called the 'Battle on the Border'. Moama would provide their artificial carpet green as practice for the Commonwealth Games, although it was a much faster surface than what was expected for India.

Straight from the heart, Rex Johnston gave an emotional, yet very honest speech prior to naming the sides. He told everyone how hard it was to pick combinations with so many great players in the squad. He said that many of us would be disappointed but should not be disheartened. The team for the England series in no way suggested the team for the Commonwealth Games, but it was to be tested against quality opposition to see how it went.

He read out the names and combinations of the side and BANG! I made it! I was selected to lead for Mark Jacobsen in the pairs. I was officially going to be an Australian player! I was going to get a green and gold cap with my unique number, and a gold uniform all my own. All the match play, training, and hard work over the years, had just paid off. It was all set for February 2010, just three weeks after I'd turn 28 years old. I was in the prime of my bowling career.

All I was worried about between that camp and my debut, was staying as healthy as possible. I hadn't at all been well during the summer, but leaving my job at Brighton allowed me to get the rest I needed to play bowls. My mental shortfalls were very rare on the green. They were mostly when I was sitting or laying down, thinking of the great, wide world.

Not many people had played lawn bowls for Australia, so I wasn't about to hand back my opportunity. I was going to enjoy every minute of my time on the greens and appreciate the sport for what it had given me. I would train the house down when I could, forgoing much of the Christmas and New Years festivities to rest, sleep, and train. All my energy went to being prepared for that match against England. It was the opportunity of a lifetime and I felt I deserved it.

If only I was healthy.

CHAPTER 30

#132

The Australian Open in Shepparton that February was a good lead up to my Australian match. I led for Neville Rodda in the pairs, preparing for my lead role at Moama. We made the quarter final in the pairs, and I also made the quarter final of the singles. My form was good.

We had to use green bowls with yellow speckles for the televised matches against England, so I made sure I used them at the Australian Open in the lead up. They were the same size and make as my last set, but for some reason they ran a narrower line. I didn't let it worry me too much, although I was still more comfortable with my normal set of bowls.

After the Australian Open concluded, we went straight to Moama for the series against England. The TV rink played host to the main game, while other 'un-capped' practice matches took place on the adjacent rinks. Jacobsen and I were confident in our match against Mark Bantock and Robert Newman, knowing we hadn't lost a single pairs match in the past two squad camps. He too liked full-length ends, so we were a great pairs combination.

Prior to the match, I was presented with my Australian Cap. To my delight, Robert Middleton had made the trip up from Melbourne to be there. He was given the duty of presenting me with my first Australian cap. Bob had been there at many special times in my bowling career, so I was thrilled that he was chosen to present me with my cap. The fact he made the effort to be there purely for my presentation, was a sign of just how wonderful he really was.

Being just two hours from my family home in Melton, Moama was a great location for my debut. It allowed them all to travel up the highway to be there as my support crew. Two car loads also made the effort to come from Brighton to support, so I knew I wasn't alone. The people who were closest to me were by my side and the stage was set for a magnificent show.

As we got our bowls out for the two-end roll-up, I felt a tear roll down my left cheek. At 28 years of age, I had been bowling for almost 16 years and it all came down to this one match. Would I sink or swim?

My single tear was not for sadness, it was for joy. I had suffered so much mentally over the past six or seven years and couldn't believe my dream of playing for Australia had finally arrived. It was going to be impossible to play the game with a clear mind. Too many things were bouncing around in my head, and I knew they would be difficult to stop. I took the mindset to play my first game as though it would be my last. I was going to enjoy every second of the experience and savour it for a lifetime. I even decided to play in my Australian cap, even though I never normally played wearing a cap.

To say I had stage fright was the understatement of the century. My leading in the first set was full of nerves, dropping short far too often for the three-bowl format. I wasn't doing my job and gave Mark no chance to save the poor head lies. I was on the main stage and was failing miserably.

We were thrashed in the first set and Mark called me up to have a quiet chat. He told me that the first set was gone, but the match wasn't. All we had to do was to scrape through the second set and get to a tiebreaker. Once there, anything could happen in three ends. He also changed our game plan by getting me to roll short jacks. At least this way I wouldn't play so many short bowls and he would have a better chance of converting heads.

I was much more relaxed during the second set. I played much better, matching or beating Bantock, on most ends. We took a three-shot lead into the last end of the second set and under pressure, I failed with my three lead bowls. By the time Mark was playing his last bowl, we were four down on the head. We could afford to drop two shots to win the set, but a drawn set or set loss, and we would lose.

After missing his drive with his second bowl, his third bowl would be our last hope of saving the match. His drive was always in the area when he let it go. The question was whether he could take out at least two of the bowls or not. Often, on an artificial surface, a bowl would skid or slide when it made contact and leave the head without touching any other bowl. "Two of them!" I screamed out as his bowl hit the head. To my delight and relief, two English shots vanished from the head, and we won the set by a single shot. It was tiebreaker time.

We won the first end of the tiebreaker but lost the second end. At 1-1 playing the final end, I knew that by winning that end, we would book ourselves a plane ticket to India for the Commonwealth Games. Bantock drove with his third bowl and despite being narrow, got a lucky bounce and made shot. My final bowl pushed Bantock's bowl out of the head, and we lay two shots on the crossover.

The target was juicy, and Englishman Newman drove at the head. He killed the end, and it was re-spotted. To our dismay, the re-spot mark lay just 18 inches away from an errant Bantock lead bowl. Jacobsen had three attempts to beat that English bowl to get us to India.

Cloud came over the green and as with that type of artificial surface, the green speed increased immediately. Jacobsen was quick with his first, which was understandable under the conditions. His second attempt was short, and he only had one rock left to save us. His final bowl looked closer but held on a track and collected Newman's short bowl. It stopped agonisingly short of shot, and the game was sadly lost.

I held my head high after the game. I was obviously disappointed that we lost, but my adrenaline was still high after playing my first match for Australia. I summarised my performance in cricket terms. My first set was like copping a 'jaffa' of a delivery and nicking it to the keeper for a duck. My second set was a fighting innings where I made a gritty and hard-fought 50. My tiebreaker was good, but not enough to get the win. All in all, it was a below average performance, but an experience that would make me a better bowler in the future.

When the Commonwealth Games side was picked just weeks later, both Jacobsen and I were left out. It was heart-breaking at the time, knowing how close we were to making the side.

As it turned out, the Indian artificial carpets were incredibly slow. They were lucky to be between 10 and 11 seconds, far from the cry of the Moama 15-16 second surface. The 'dead' tracks would have been perfect for Jacobsen and me to play our long ends. We missed out on a great opportunity.

The Australian men and women failed to win a single gold medal in lawn bowls at the 2010 Delhi Games. There were three silvers and a bronze, but in terms of the expectations of our Australian players, it was sighted as a disappointing performance. It resulted in the resignation of National Coach Rex Johnston and some of the high-performance staff. Zero gold medals meant there had to be a change at the helm.

Jacobsen and I still stake claim that if he drew that last shot, we would have played the pairs for Australia in Delhi. It was not only a depressing experience to miss the trip, but it also felt even worse watching the Australian team play their guts out for no ultimate glory.

The 22nd of February 2010 was not only my first capped game for Australia, but also my last. Fourteen years later, I never experienced the privilege of playing again for our magnificent country. I will always be known as 'one-time Jackaroo Lee Schraner', a label I despise. Yes, it was an honour to represent my country in the sport, but to hear 'one-time' is a constant reminder of all the games I could have played if given the opportunity. If only Jacobsen had just drawn that last shot.

But that's bowls.

CHAPTER 31

One

I was lucky enough to qualify for the Professional Bowls Association (PBA) Scottish Open in November, played in Perth, Scotland. Drawing number one seed Nick Brett in the first round should have sent me home packing, but I was determined to at least be competitive. Not only did I give him a tough match, but I also knocked him out in straight sets. The high would be short-lived as another Englishman, Ian Bond, would take me out in the second round. It was a hell of a trip though. I got to see some beautiful buildings and sites, making the most of my remaining days away.

Not long after that, Neville and I teamed up in the NSW Open at Wagga Wagga, making it all the way to the pairs final. Despite keeping Aaron Wilson and Matt Flapper scoreless in the second set, our first set loss meant we had to go to a tiebreaker. After the three ends, we were tied and had to play an extra end. Unfortunately, Wilson and Flapper were too good, and we had to settle for silver. It was the furthest we had been in a Grand Prix Open, but previous consistent results saw us climb to the number one and two ranked pairs players in Australia.

The Australian Open 2011 was in February at Darebin City. Direct entries were cut to only a handful, and Neville and I were not included in those entries, forced to go through qualifying in Bendigo to make the main draw. I thought it was ridiculous at the time considering our Australian rankings, with the blazers naming mostly Australian players and Internationals as the direct entries. I was also forced to qualify in the singles and triples, even though my ranking in both those disciplines was much higher than many of the pre-selected entries. If I wanted to play in the Australian Open at Darebin, I had to fight my way through qualification for everything.

After three days in Bendigo and 12 straight wins, I finally earned a place in the main draw of all three disciplines. Darebin City was a lot different to playing in Bendigo. The greens were International length (40 metres) and generally 4-5 seconds slower. I loved playing at Darebin though because it suited my game plan perfectly. I could have 36-metre-long ends on unpredictable and slow greens – all challenges that I loved. Using my draw/drive game was best when a green wasn't perfect. Many opponents would try and use in between weight with very little success.

The first week of the main draw started perfectly. I got through the first round of every discipline, lining up some harder round two fixtures. In the pairs, Neville and I beat Gary Lawson and Shannon McIlroy in straight sets, putting us through to the last 16 against Anthony Kiepe and Nathan Rice. We also got through to the last 16 of the triples, facing English Internationals Stuart Airey, Mervyn King and Australian, John Green. I was also through to the last 16 of the singles, having wins against Mac Maclean and Queensland Open singles champion, Paul Jopson. I went into week two of the Australian Open alive in every event.

After beating Brett Wilkie in the last 16 of the singles, Neville and I got past Kiepe and Rice in the pairs in straight sets. In the triples, we played our best game yet, outing Green and the English Internationals. Onto the quarter finals.

My run ended in the singles when the young whippersnapper Aaron Wilson, took me apart in straight sets. I remember telling many around the green that morning, that this kid was going to be a star. My prediction was spot on, seeing him go to the greatest heights in the sport over the next decade.

We won our quarter final in the triples against the star-studded trio of David Ferguson, Matt Pieterson, and Carl Healey, setting up a semi-final against Brett Wilkie, Wayne Turley, and Aron Sheriff.

Neville and I scraped past Daniel Woodrow and Mark Johnston from Essendon in the pairs quarter final, drawing the second set to claim victory. Our semi-final would be one for the ages, drawing Brett Wilkie and Leif Selby in a night match.

In pouring rain on the front green at Darebin City, Neville and I were happy to take underdog status for the semi-final of the pairs. The way we were playing, we thought we were a chance to beat anyone. We had already defeated a lot of strong combinations along the way, so in our minds, we had nothing to lose.

With Neville putting on a master display of leading, we won the match in straight sets to advance to the final. I had been there before with Mario Cipolla three years earlier, but this time felt different. I genuinely believed we could win it.

The following morning, we lost a thriller in the triples semifinal, losing on an extra end to Sheriff, Turley and Wilkie in the tie-breaker. It was only fair that Wilkie got me back in something, after I had knocked him out of both the pairs and singles. With the pairs final set for the next day, it was time to go home and rest.

Neville and I chose the bright red uniform as our television gear. Red was a colour of power and dominance, so we wanted to walk onto the rink feeling like we owned it.

We met Aron Sheriff and Mark Berghofer, the current Australian pairs combination, and our representatives in the Delhi 2010 Commonwealth Games. If we were to win it, we had to beat the best bowlers Australia could throw at us.

I struggled at the beginning of the final to find the weight of the surface. Neville and Mark were both playing well at lead, but Aron was taking me apart at skip. I couldn't smoke on the TV rink but was able to grab a puff or two behind the temporary rink walls.

When we dropped the maximum count of six in the first set, it was all but over. We lost the set by seven and had to re-focus for the second set. I was playing shit. I had to lift for us to be any chance at all. At 0-7 after three ends in the second set, the match was gone. I walked past Neville and under his breath I heard him say, "Pull your finger out, this is embarrassing". I was angry with him because we were best mates. We had to stick together through thick and thin, winning or losing. He told me after the game that he said it to fire me up. He knew I was flat and had to get me going somehow. He was right.

From end four onwards, it really was the 'Schraner show'. We clawed back to 7-8 with just two ends to go, giving us a chance to win the second set. I was comfortable on the green, feeling the weight better and having an influence on the match. On end eight, I drew a super shot around a short bowl to land right in front of the jack. Sheriff returned fire by firing a forehand shot through a small gap to clip my bowl clean out of the head. We were one down on the head and the match was on a knife's edge.

After a look around at the head, Nev and I noticed we had the three best bowls at the back of the rink. If I was able to follow the same funnel that Sheriff had just found, I could get the jack in the ditch or have it re-spotted by going out-of-bounds and could make four shots. Neville was having a look at some shot on the backhand, but my focus was solely on the forehand shot. I saw an opportunity to not only get the shot, but to make four and potentially seal the second set.

Neville looked me in the eyes and said, "What does your gut say?"

Without any hesitation, I said, "Same forehand gap as Sheriff. Jack back for four".

"Well go up there and get it kiddo", Neville responded.

The bowl in my hand was the last one of the end. After I took my stance, lined up and took a deep breath, I felt calm, relaxed, and clear-minded. I knew I just had to get it.

I was very interested when I released the bowl, knowing I was close. The bowl wasn't even halfway down the green when I yelled, "Nev! I got him Nev!" I knew I had it metres out and was screaming with delight to my pairs partner. And I got it alright. The grandstand was thumping and shaking with applause, as the jack was re-spotted for four shots.

A single on the final end of the set gave us a 12-8 win, putting us into a tiebreaker.

The first end was weird. We had a lot of close bowls, and the target was broad. Sheriff hesitated to drive and played conversion weight down the inconsistent backhand side. One held wide, one hit a short bowl, and his third and final attempt turned underneath the head. I added a couple of shots to Neville's counter, and we scored three.

The second end was a longer end and somewhat scrappy. My first two draw shot attempts fell short, leaving me with one bowl to reverse the head from one down, to one up. I drew the shot with my final rock, and despite a valiant attempt from Sheriff, he got a vile result and had to concede two shots.

Playing the last end, we were 5-0 up and surely had the title in our hands. We had already dropped a maximum six shots in that direction during the first set, so I was taking nothing for granted. We held on, dropping just a single. We were the Australian Open pairs champions!

From a set and 0-7 down, it would have been easy to give up. It was Neville's little comment during the second set that got me going. I used my fiery mood to play more aggressively, greatly influencing the result. We had our fair share of luck along the way which you need in big events. But we made the most of our performance and luck and went all the way.

There are no pictures on the scorecard.

CHAPTER 32

Flick

After pennant finished, the Victorian side went to Nelson Bay for the Alley Shield. I had remained in the side since my debut and was now up to 160 State test matches. I took a new set of bowls with me, the same make and model as my set from the Australian Open, but in my sponsors new lime fizz colour. It was a foolish move.

The Victorian side won yet another silver medal, although I didn't help much, having to borrow two of Neville's bowls to use in the championships. My new set was strangely wide – and I mean wide! I was a metre outside anyone else's grass line, finding it almost impossible to play a conversion shot. I put the set in the bin after our training day and never saw them again.

After the main event, I had the pleasure of playing singles for Victoria in the newly formed 'Super 6' competition, where each State and Territory fielded a team of triples, pairs, and a singles player. Neville wasn't in the Super 6 side but left his bowls there for me to use. Even though the bowls were a size too big and uncomfortable in my hand, I was at least competitive with them.

I led 20-13 against Mark Nitz from Tasmania (TAS) in round one, just one shot away from the target of 21. In a freak two ends, I lost the plot and conceded two maximum counts of four to lose 20-21. I was frustrated, disappointed, and angry with myself. In a tantrum, I kicked a bowl into the ditch with mighty force. I knew I'd hurt myself but crept in for lunch keeping to myself.

After lunch, I snuck outside to a quiet area and took my shoe and sock off to assess the damage. My big toe was purple and there was a lot of blood on my sock. There was no doubt I had broken it. A split-second idiotic temper burst had made a mess of my right big toe – and deservedly so. Anyone silly enough to lose their cool like I did got no sympathy for the pain.

I had two choices; I could keep it to myself and play on or tell the Victorian coach and selectors what I had done. I chose the latter but made up some excuse about tripping on the stairs after lunch. They wanted me to play rounds two and three, as substitutes weren't allowed in singles. I think they wanted me to suffer for my outburst. They weren't stupid. I'm pretty sure they knew exactly what had caused the damage, seeing me boot the bowl before lunch.

In round two I had a gutsy 21-19 win over Ashley Klose from South Australia (SA), who went on to win the gold medal. By round three, I couldn't step, so played off a fixed stance. A young Anthony Provost from Western Australia (WA) wiped me off the rink. I was copping all the pain I deserved.

I ended up playing off for 5th and 6th against the Northern Territory (NT) and won comfortably 21-9. It was a good finish to the tournament, but a huge failure by my singles standard.

When flying home, I was startled by the thought of the State singles and State Champion of Champions singles finals being just a week away. I didn't own a set of bowls, had a broken toe, and lost all confidence in Nelson Bay. It was a worrying situation.

I went straight to the doctors when I got home. An X-ray showed that I had broken my toe in two places. I had an injection so I could walk properly, had it supported by a splint, and scored some decent pain killers on prescription. I was planning for the upcoming State championships and pain killers would be my saving grace.

Geoff helped me out with a set of bowls from his bowls shop. I didn't have enough time to get a new set from my sponsors, so had to make do with what was available. It was a big risk taking a new set with me, but at least the set were the right size and held a tighter line than my last lot of bowls.

I arrived in Wangaratta the day before the State singles was due to start. To my relief, the set of bowls from the shop had a great grass line and I picked up their trajectory almost straight away.

You would think that after so many years of bowls that I'd have played in the State singles finals a few times before. This was untrue. I had been successful in Champion of Champions singles before, but never the State singles. It was the first time I had ever got past the region stage in the event.

I got through the round of 16 against Graeme Gebus from Bundoora RSL, lining up a quarter final with John Clarke from Edithvale. The greens were speeding up and my toe was giving me grief. It was a careful balance between pain and taking pain killers; too many pain killers and I would lose the feel of the bowl in my hand, too few and I would be in extraordinary pain.

At 12-19 down, a friendly spectator told me that he'd back me to get the 13 I needed, before John could score his six. I dug deep and found the will to comeback and win 25-22. Talk about a massive relief to get through the first day.

The semi-final against Rowan Sharpe from Burwood was far more comfortable, getting the job done 25-15. The State final was against Nathan Bush from Geelong, with tactics a huge factor in the match. I wanted long ends, and he wanted the shortest length possible. He was backhand dominant, and I was forehand dominant. It must have been amazing to watch. Two guys going hammer and tong in a State final with absolutely no regard for what the other player was doing. We had our own game plans and theories and were going to stick to them no matter what. It was awesome.

In a great match, I saluted 25-19 to win my first State singles. I couldn't celebrate too hard as my favourite event, the Champion of Champions singles, was due to start the next morning.

I got through the round of 16 match against Frank Seaton from Corowa 25-16 to set up a re-match with an old friend from a decade earlier, John Leitch from Mulgrave. It was time to test my new style of singles against the man who showed me the light when we last played in Trafalgar. We threw ditch to ditch lengths against each other for 25 consecutive ends, with neither player willing to steer away from their game plan. This time, I was ready for the challenge and stormed away with a 25-12 scorecard.

The other three left in the championship included Mark Ryan from Mooroopna, and strangely enough, two men named Wayne Roberts, one from City Oval Ballarat, and the other, my State skipper.

My semi-final against 'Ballarat Wayne' was a non-event, and in just over an hour I was in the clubhouse with a 25-6 victory. If I wanted to win my third State Champion of Champions singles, I had to once again beat my State skipper who accounted for Mark Ryan 25-20. Our last match in Swan Hill a few years earlier was a cracker, but in a nutshell, it had nothing on this epic battle.

Seven hours, 34 ends, three rain delays, and a soaked Wangaratta track all featured in the final. During rain delays, the greenkeepers were pushing water off the green with specialised brooms. Every time we stopped, I got more nervous. I could win a unique double here and etch my name in the history books alongside Bill Cornehls and Glyn Bosisto, the only other two players in 130 years to have achieved the feat. I wanted it so bad.

In a tense and thrilling final finished under lights, I hung on to win the match 25-23. My mission was completed, and I was now the best singles player in Victoria without doubt. These victories would do my Australian squad chances no harm at all.

Or so I thought.

In the space of less than two months, I had won the Australian Open Pairs gold medal, the Victorian State singles gold medal, and the Victorian Champion of Champions singles gold medal. I was ranked number one in Australia in singles and pairs and looking forward to another year in the Australian squad.

Just six days after my success in Wangaratta, I was telephoned by the new Australian Coach, Steve Glasson. He took the top job after Rex Johnston stepped down following the Delhi Commonwealth Games.

Don't get me wrong, Steve was one of the best bowlers this country had ever produced. His knowledge of players across Australia was second to none and his record at World Bowls and Commonwealth Games was astonishing.

But, just five years earlier, he was on the television show 'A Current Affair', negatively highlighting the new Australian high-performance program and fitness regime. He had missed selection for the Commonwealth Games in Melbourne 2006, so made the decision to go National on his thoughts of the new setup. His story sent shockwaves through the bowling world and made Bowls Australia appear to be inept and deranged. Now, like it never even happened, here he was as the National Coach and head of the program.

Surely someone was having me on.

How was this even possible?

During the call, we talked about the Commonwealth Games, World Bowls, Asia Pacific Championships, and other major events in the future. The only problem for me was that after deliberation, I wasn't going to be a part of it. The Australian selectors had named their new squad internally and before announcing it to the public, omitted players had to be called.

To mine, and many other people's shock, I was no longer an Australian squad member. To add to further disappointment, I wasn't even named in the second-tier Australian squad, nor the development team. I had been omitted completely from all Australian squad calculations.

What a kick in the guts!

I always believed that selection was a matter of opinion and that results meant everything. In essence, if you kept winning major titles you would automatically pick yourself without argument. I'd won more State titles in the last five years than any other male bowler in Australia. I had attended every Grand Prix event on the calendar, winning two gold medals and two silver medals in the process. I was the number one ranked bowler in the country in singles and pairs and had done all the drills and paperwork I was told to do. And yet, all of this would mean nothing.

My mental health had improved dramatically over the past few months, but this squad omission would trigger frequent bouts of anxiety and depression. I was angry. I thought the non-selection was a total joke. Here I was at the top of my game, producing massive results consistently, only to be snubbed by the National selectors. At 29 years of age, I knew it would be an uphill battle to get back into the squad. With a focus on the younger generation apparent, my chances of ever getting back in the green and gold would fade with age.

I really wanted to take the best in the world on. I wanted to win World and Commonwealth medals. I wanted to be on the dais singing 'Advance Australia Fair'. I wanted it all, but it wasn't going to happen. My one match against England in 2010 would be the only capped game I'd ever play. My National career was effectively over. In my mind, they were totally wrong but there was nothing I could do about it. It was a gross injustice.

It was time for a shock announcement.

CHAPTER 33

Thirty

Neville and I had started our new partnership in the business world, operating a boutique web design business. We also had other start-ups and business ventures on the go. If I couldn't get a job working for a boss, the only way I was going to make an income was to work for myself.

It changed my life in many ways. It gave me a lot of things to look forward to that had nothing to do with lawn bowls. Once omitted from the Australian squad, my goals in sport were replaced by goals in the business world. I was reasonably healthy and could devote day and night to the new businesses, now free from the huge calendar of commitment to lawn bowls.

My decision to retire from State and National duties wasn't as tough as many other people thought it was. In my mind, I believed I was good enough to be in the Australian team, but with the lack of support from the selectors, I decided to pull the pin on it all. If I wasn't going to make the squad at the peak of my life and powers, how would I ever make it in the future? Less than a year away from turning 30, I decided it was time to set myself up financially for the future. I had no assets to show for myself other than a car, and even that was on finance.

Bowls saved my life through my twenties, but it also slowed my life down. It cost me more money to play than I ever made, and with up to 15 weeks a year off for major events, it was impossible to get a decent job – even though I was healthy. So, I turned to business development and building successful corporate partnerships. I was enjoying it immensely and felt that it would be my future. Bowls took a backseat role in life. I hardly put a bowl down that winter.

My announcement started many feeds on social media sites around the world. Many said I was snubbed because I was Victorian. Others said I was snubbed because I was gay. I didn't want to think about any of it to be honest. I was firm on my decision and didn't want it to distract me from my new goals. All I planned to do was play pennant at Brighton. I didn't even enter a single club event or State event, willing to give up my chance of defending my two singles crowns.

By the start of the 2011/12 pennant season, we had recruited well and after previous failures, we had our mind set on a division one premiership and promotion into premier division. Neville Rodda had joined us, as well as Phil Ashman from Karingal, Rob Huddle, and other solid players.

Neville and I rented an apartment in St Kilda together to be closer to the city. It was easier to visit clients and network, being so close to the CBD. It wasn't cheap, but with two of us paying rent, it was affordable. By living together, we were able to get much more work done.

The pennant season was unbelievable, as we dominated the division right up to Christmas. It would be an epic failure from the club not to make it into premier division. Unfortunately, during the mid-season break, Neville found a girl and moved out of the apartment. I was left to pay the whole rent of $440 a week by myself. This was well-outside my budget, so I took in a boarder to help with the expenses.

My 30th birthday that January was a celebration of many things. I made it a fancy-dress party, and everyone turned up as their favourite musicians. I came as John Lennon, fully dressed in a kaftan, wig, and glasses, only because I couldn't find a Roy Orbison costume.

I invited everyone I knew. We had about 70 guests in all, having a ball in the Parkview Room at the Brighton Bowling Club. My favourite songs of all time were belting loudly, and I was consuming a beverage or twelve.

There was one special guest at the party that no-one knew except me. I knew him extremely well and he certainly knew me better than anyone else in the room.

He was the man I saw many times during my nervous breakdown. The man who went out of his way to help a struggling young male cope with his mental health demons. The man who saw me at my lowest and most vulnerable. The man who at first, mainly due to my costume, didn't recognise a healthy me.

It was my doctor.

I had an elephant-like memory and when sending out birthday invitations, I recalled the moment he told me I'd be lucky to make it to 30. I didn't know if he would come, but I'm so glad he did.

As he approached me, I removed my wig and glasses. I held one hand out to shake his hand, and the other outstretched to the side for a hug. He looked me up and down and couldn't help but smile. What we said to each other wasn't important. It was about the physical contact and for him to see how far I'd come since that horrific time. It was a very emotional embrace for me, and I couldn't help but cry. I felt an overwhelming sense of satisfaction and achievement. What I had been through that past nine years was nothing short of a nightmare, but I was still there, still fighting, still existing.

My birthday fizzled out late in the night and everyone that came had a blast. The booze flowed, the people danced, and the whole celebration was amazing. The speeches by my parents, Neville, and Geoff, were all very generous. A lot of people there learnt something new about who I was and what I had achieved in life. It was a night I will never forget.

Brighton dominated the division one competition and had a massive win over Mentone in the grand final played at Yarraville/Footscray. On a pristine grass surface, we flew out of the blocks and were never headed, going on to win by 47 shots overall. Both us and Mentone were promoted into Premier Division.

My lease expired in St Kilda and I couldn't wait to move. Two members at Brighton organised a penthouse on Hotham Street, less than two kilometres from where I was previously living, completely rent free for me and Brighton's newest recruit for premier division, Aaron Wilson.

We had many great times in that place, but our stay would only last six months. The two members at Brighton had a fallout, and consequently, we were evicted immediately.

I moved back in with my parents. My two brothers and sister had moved out of home, so I had a whole room to myself. I set up a home office and also got to spend a lot of quality time with mum and dad. We had hardly seen each other for the past decade, so catching up with them was overdue.

My parents were an inspiration for me as a child and when moving back home, they continued to be that rock for me. You would think that moving back home at 30 years of age was taking a backward step, but sometimes you had to take a step back in order to move forward. The 60-kilometre trip to Brighton didn't really bother me because I loved the club. The distance was no problem with decent music on the radio while cruising down the highway.

I played in the Victorian Open in Shepparton after ignoring the event in its inaugural year in 2011. I earnt the nickname, 'Marathon Man', after playing 33 games in six days. I won the gold medal with Aaron Wilson in the pairs, another gold with Gayle Edwards in the mixed pairs, and lost a thrilling singles final to Mark Ryan, winning a silver medal.

The Victorian Open destroyed me physically and mentally in 2012. My efforts had me roll-up some mornings at 7:45am, finishing under lights well after midnight the next morning. My blisters were so bad on my feet, that I was forced to place them in a bucket of water to get my socks off. The blood and pus from broken blisters made my skin stick to my socks. It was very painful. The six-day schedule was eventually extended to ensure that no-one would ever go through that type of week again. The 'Vic Medal' was also established shortly after, for the best player at the event. Tournament director Barbara Gilbert told me the award was created because of my efforts in 2012. I didn't return to the event until 2016.

Our start in premier division was a success, winning enough matches to be free of the relegation zone by Christmas. We were even a sneaky chance for finals in our first season.

Around this time, I was in negotiations with Kew Heights about a future job and coaching deal. They were about to merge with the Melbourne Cricket Club Bowling Club (MCC) and would have access to a lot more funds. The offer was substantial, and I was planning on taking it at the end of the current season.

I found a place in Alphington and decided to move out of home for the second time. Alphington was close to Kew and rumours started to circle about why I was living in Alphington and playing at Brighton, which were miles apart across town. I even got a part-time bookkeeping job in Auburn Road, Hawthorn, as the businesses were only earning sporadic income. We were spending too much time and money on one start-up and not doing enough with our income-generating businesses. I had no choice but to find work.

Unfortunately, after the Christmas break, Brighton lost couple of matches at home and finished the season in sixth. It was by no means a disaster. Every team's goal their first year in the premier division was to survive. However, we did blow a genuine chance to make the final four.

Maybe next season.

CHAPTER 34

Circles

Neville and I had a massive fallout over winter. It was during a trip to Borneo that we argued about the dedication of each partner to our businesses. In the end, we made a sensible decision to dissolve the partnership. Each of us took half of the portfolio and registered them as sole proprietorships. It had an impact on our friendship, but knowing how close we were deep down, it would survive in the long run.

I was the sole trader of GenZ Web Solutions and Barefoot at Brighton, with a new registration pending for LJ Schraner Group. My ambition was to build a complete portfolio of businesses, get them off the ground, and then hire staff and management to run the daily operations. I was looking for multiple streams of income where I could continually expand the portfolio. Many of the richest people in the world had that style of income stream. Richard Branson comes to mind.

If a business failed, I would deregister it and start on a new idea. I was able to build cheap websites with my computer knowledge and had no problems doing the business administration and accounts. I was able to work from home and do my own hours. It was a sensational idea.

With business going well, I found enough free time to rekindle some old friendships and to spend quality time with the people I loved. Everything seemed to be on track.

It was an emotional phone call from Victorian Chairman of Selectors, and great friend, John Gullan, that put my life in a spin once more. In a private discussion, he said things to me that meant a hell of a lot. He told me that by retiring, I had let go of a chance to become the greatest bowler Victoria ever had. He was honest and frank and told me of his disappointment and disgust of my retirement. He insisted that I was greatly missed, and Victoria needed me back if we were going to threaten for the Alley Shield. As a friend, he asked if I was seriously interested in making a comeback.

I didn't decide straight away with fear of not thinking it through. It took me a week or so before I decided to call him back. I was worried about the backlash I'd cop from people around the bowling community. To me, it would be embarrassing to be gone for good one minute, then back the next. It took a great man like Gullan to influence me, but I decided to make a comeback.

I got nicknames like 'Farnham' and 'Kotter' from my team-mates when I returned. The comments were all in gest and for a laugh, so I'd laugh along with them. It was a great feeling to pull on the 'Big V' once more and even better to rejoin a partnership with my old skip, Wayne Roberts.

Sometimes you sit back and realise a decision you made was wrong. I knew after playing State bowls again that my decision to retire was a poor one. My love for the game, my teammates, the people around the sport, and all those other good things, were certainly missed. Playing for Victoria was an opportunity and honour that many bowlers didn't get. It was a privilege to don the navy-blue uniform and represent the State with pride. I couldn't help but appreciate the fact that I once let this go and was lucky enough to get it back. I would never do it again. I would play State bowls forever, as long as I could keep up with the level required. I was in for the long haul and determined to rack up as many representative games as I could. I also wanted that elusive Alley Shield gold medal.

I also notified Bowls Australia that I was available again for National selection.

I was asked by Bowls Victoria to become an ambassador for their newly formed partnership with *beyondblue*, a support centre for those who suffered from mental health problems. Now that I had learned to live with depression and anxiety, I felt I could contribute to society by helping those at the peak of their suffering. I was always on social media during the day with work, so I was available to talk with anyone who felt the need to reach out.

It was amazing how many bowlers I spoke to. Many found it comforting to talk with me on a chat screen, rather than having to speak the actual words. I often told them my story of suffering and how I eventually learnt to live with mental illness, although I had some serious hurdles along the way. I still talk to people today online, hopeful that our chats have a benefit on their lives.

I knew a lot about the debilitating illness and how it affected every area of my life. It was time for me to give back to a society that gave me so much when I was at my lowest.

It was the least I could do.

CHAPTER 35

Bradleigh

During State champions week in April, I once again had the opportunity to win the State Champion of Champions singles. After getting through my region with a 25-24 final win over Giora Pomerantz, the dream of a fourth gold medal in the event was in sight.

After three competitive matches, including an awesome contest with Matt Flapper, I found myself in the State final against who else, but Wayne Roberts. At Bendigo East in the Autumn sun, we put on another epic display of singles bowling. I won the final couple of ends to claim a 25-20 win over my good mate and toss the mat into the afternoon sky once more. A fourth crown put me just three behind Bosisto. At 31 years of age, I had plenty of time to catch him.

The Kew deal fell through, and I was stuck with a lease in Alphington. My enthusiastic approach to the potential new club and income had got me in a sticky situation. The area wasn't cheap to live in which wouldn't have been an issue if I got the new contract. Unfortunately for me, I ended up miles away from my home club Brighton, paying a rent I couldn't really afford on my income.

One August night while sitting in my armchair watching the AFL football, I had a knock on my door. It was unusual for anyone to knock on my door at all unless it was a postman, but there were no postmen at 9:30pm in the evening.

I opened the door and there stood 17-year-old Bradleigh Griffiths looking disturbed and extremely upset. Without saying a word, I let him in and offered him something to drink. He sat on the couch obviously in distress and I couldn't help but ask why he was here.

Brad and his father often had fallouts. They both lived with his grandmother in Hurstbridge and this closer contact only led to more heated exchanges. With Brad almost fully grown, it wasn't uncommon for their arguments to get physical and abusive. He had been kicked out of home and needed somewhere to stay.

My Alphington apartment was a shoebox. It was a one-bedroom 'motel-style' set up with kitchenette and ensuite bathroom. I simply didn't have the space or money to take Brad in, but he had nowhere else to go. It was either make room for him or send him out into the night homeless and frightened. I'd been there before and wouldn't wish it on my worst enemy, so I took him in. I made room. I made him feel welcome.

I had known Brad for several years. He came to watch me play bowls from time to time and we would often have a chat.

Back in the Bundoora days, I had a short relationship with a guy that I later found out was Brad's father. Although he had two sons, his dad had been in denial about his sexuality and was finally exploring his true feelings. The young boys running around the Greensborough unit were Brad and his brother. Brad had made the connection earlier than I did and it was highly embarrassing for the both of us. He was old enough to remember my face, and after starting bowls himself and seeing that I was a bowler, was able to join the dots.

Was Brad knocking on my door because he needed a new father figure?

I treated him like a son, but also a mate. I got him bowling at Brighton and he impressed in the practice matches, starting as a lead in our premier division team. Still being a child, I was responsible for getting him to and from the club for training and pennant matches.

When Brad turned 18 that September, we had a massive night at my local drinking hole. It might have been a Tuesday night, but it didn't stop us from over-indulging in schooners of Carlton Draught with a dash of raspberry cordial. The heavy beers hit us hard and it took us a good couple of days to recover.

I gave Brad some work at Barefoot at Brighton helping with functions. I also gave work to Daniel Hudson and Aaron Wilson, the fastest dishwasher I had ever seen. Heading into the warmer weather, I needed helping hands to deal with the huge list of booked events.

That October, while sitting in my apartment with Brad, I got another late-night knock at the door. Standing at the door was Daniel, with those all-familiar facial expressions that I had seen with Brad just two months earlier. I let him in the door and offered him something to drink. He parked himself on the couch next to Brad, looking disturbed and eerily quiet.

Daniel was a couple of years older than Brad, but immature for his age. Brad had learned to grow up fast through family separation, while Daniel had been nurtured by his mum and grandmother, Victorian and Australian bowling legend, Gordana Baric.

It wasn't me who spoke first this time. Daniel simply sat on the couch, a blank look in his eyes, saying he too had been kicked out of home. I had become the half-way house of young men with nowhere to go. Knowing he wouldn't last on the street; I allowed him to stay. I didn't care how crammed my apartment was, I wasn't going to let Daniel experience the loneliness and depression of homelessness. I was his last resort.

With functions going well, I didn't have to charge the boys any rent or utilities. The work I gave them provided the pocket money they needed to play bowls tournaments and pennant. Life was tight for them, but they had enough to get by.

It was a November pennant match against Mentone that changed the course of our three lives. We thrashed them at home in a spiteful match, where just one more player boil-over could have seen an all-in-brawl. Our rivalry had gone too far and although we were victorious, my love for the sport was dissipating. Brighton was on top of the premier division ladder and yet, I was not enjoying my pennant bowls at all. I thought about pulling the pin completely and having some time away from the greens.

I made a crazy decision straight out of leftfield. After talking with my mate Josh Tegg from Glenorchy-Rodman bowls club in Hobart, I told the boys that I had decided to move to Tasmania. They could either come with me or had to find a new place to live. I was leaving Melbourne in the first week of January 2014, selling my business and making a fresh start. I needed to find the love for bowls again, even if that meant moving states. I was over the intensity and 'win at all costs' attitude of the Melbourne premier division and wanted out.

To my surprise, both the boys said they would come with me. It was clear they needed a fresh start just like me. I immediately found a rental property in Claremont with three bedrooms. The size of the property was a welcomed relief from what we had been living in, even if it was a little old and neglected. To seal the lease on the property, the boys had to go before Christmas. I'd finish off the functions at Brighton, finalise the sale of my business, and join them in January.

My decision to leave did have its consequences. I'd have to leave my bookkeeping job, sell a thriving barefoot bowls business, tell my teammates I was leaving them, and somehow explain to my family that I was moving interstate. None of these were easy, but I was firm on my decision to leave. I also had to let the Victorian selectors know I was moving away and could potentially be competition for them in the future. After 206 games for my beloved home state, I was leaving their strength and depth to join a minnow state.

In the first week of January, I drove to Station Pier in Port Melbourne and boarded the Spirit of Tasmania to Devonport. I booked a room and took the night run, able to sleep most of the 12-hour trip. It was dark as the boat departed Melbourne. I made my way to the rear of the vessel, lit up a smoke, and stood on the decking outside. The lights from the city and apartment buildings along the shore were breathtaking.

When my smoke reached the filter, I'd throw it away and light another one. All I could do was stare back at the shore, until the lights eventually faded away over the horizon. I don't know if it was the beautiful view, the emotion of leaving Melbourne behind, or the fear of making a new life in Tasmania, but I was overwhelmed with emotion. My tears were quickly dried by the fresh, cool breeze sweeping across the boat. It was the freezing air that knocked me to my senses, as I said goodbye to Victoria. I began to let go, as I walked to the door allowing me inside the cabin. I opened the door slowly with my head bowed, taking in a long, deep breath.

I turned and looked again.

CHAPTER 36

Tassie

The boat docked in Devonport, and I had a three-hour drive ahead to Claremont. I messaged the boys telling them I had arrived in Tasmania and was in my car on the way. I had been to Tasmania a few times before for both bowls and holidays. If it weren't for the miserable weather, I could easily move back there in a heartbeat. In my opinion, it was the most beautiful state in Australia.

I arrived late morning to Chippendale Street, Claremont. The boys came running out of the house as my BMW pulled up in the driveway. There were smiles and hugs all around, realising our dream of moving to Tasmania together had come to fruition. After unloading the car, I went straight to the second-hand furniture shop in Moonah to buy a bed. The boys had already organised the other appliances we needed, with me sending money from Melbourne as required.

Next it was off to the bowling club in Glenorchy to have a beer and catch up with Josh. When we arrived, the State fours final was being played so we all started watching it. After grabbing a jug of beer and some glasses, I sat outside and lit a smoke.

My first real communication with Grant Allford was not a positive one. As umpire, he marched over as the 'smoke police' and told me to put it out immediately or go outside the club gate. I didn't know that Tasmanian sporting clubs had become 100% smoke-free and that I had to be outside the club to smoke. Had I known that before moving, I might have changed my mind!

Grant and I became very close friends over the next five years. Not only did we win two State triples gold medals together, but we also played pennant in the same rink for a while. Being an ex VFL (now AFL) footballer with Richmond in the 1970's, Grant was a dominant figure. He had authority and was a stickler for the rules, but deep-down he was a top bloke. When you went into battle, you wanted him on your side. I always made fun of his age to make him laugh and relax. Being in his late 60's, I couldn't help but give him the nickname 'bag', short for 'colostomy bag'. It stuck, and I still call him by the same nickname today.

The guys around the club had already seen Brad and Daniel bowl several times. Many of them stayed back after the State fours final to see me roll-up for the first time. The green was incredibly slow compared to what I was used to at Brighton, reminding me immediately of my days at Karingal. Within a few ends, I picked up the weight and line and started popping bowls all over the jack. I'd then throw down a forehand thunderbolt and hit the jack or the head of bowls. There was excitement in the air.

My first game for Glenorchy-Rodman was a big win against Sandy Bay away. I was skipping a rink and had Josh, Daniel, and Anthony Clifford. Our side was on top of the ladder and clear favourites to win the premiership. The inclusion of us three boys from Melbourne made the team almost unbackable in every match we played.

That evening, while drinking at the club, we were invited on the green to experience our initiation. The club religiously welcomed members through a ritual, asking them to join the 'Punja tribe'. The tribal name had no relation to any aboriginal communities or any other groups of people from around the world, it was simply club's made-up cultural brotherhood. To be welcomed into the tribe meant you became one of the brothers and could partake in war with the club on the bowling green.

I'll be honest. When the boundary pegs were pulled out of the bank by tribal leaders and they started clapping them and chanting, I was petrified! Us three boys were in the middle of a huddle of club members who all chanted together. It was a strange, yet honourable experience. Some of the chanting was so funny that I burst into laughter. It was in that moment I knew I had made the right choice to come to Tasmania.

Just weeks after arriving, I was named as a skip in the Tasmanian Men's side, as well as getting the singles discipline in the Super 6's tournament. My selection created a lot of conjecture and controversy around the State. Some of the players who missed the team had been trying their guts out for years to be selected, and in less than a month I had been given the opportunity. I didn't know how to react to the social media comments and gossip, other than to go out there and play the best bowls I could.

The following week I entered the Southern Singles, a tournament for all players from any club in Hobart. I won my way through to the final, went up that weekend to win the Penguin Pairs with Aaron Wilson, only to come back and beat Cameron Tegg in a classic. After winning both Tasmania's most prestigious tournament and the Southern singles crown, the online comments seemed to stop. I had earnt the trust and respect of Tasmanian bowlers.

The few months us three had together in Tasmania is mostly blurry. I'd missed partying in my 20's due to ill health, so I was planning to make up for it. The boys didn't have much money after rent and bills, so I found myself loading up the fridge for the three of us to drink. I don't think we were sober for three months, certainly living up our time on the Apple Isle.

Glenorchy-Rodman made the grand final of pennant, only to see it delayed due to the timing of the Alley Shield. Although at South

Burnie, the timing of the Nationals meant we would have to wait 22 days to play in the grand final.

In the Super 6's, I won my three sectional matches against Scott Thulborn, Aron Sheriff, and Anthony Kiepe, to set up a gold medal playoff against Victorian Dylan Fisher. He was far too good for me in the final, winning 21-13 and taking the gold.

The Alley shield was a stepping stone for Tasmania, beating the NT, SA and WA. A close loss against the Australian Capital Territory (ACT) meant we finished 5th, where as a win would have seen us climb to third. It was Tasmania's best result at an Alley Shield for some years, so the feeling among the State team was positive moving forward.

The pennant grand final was a disaster, losing a last end thriller to Rosny Park. We were clear favourites going into the match, but several poor player performances opened the door to an upset. To Rosny's credit, they took advantage of our below-par performance and snatched the grand final from our fingertips. It made a special season turn into a very sombre night. It was a sad finish for a side who dominated the entire competition, only to put in a poor performance on the biggest stage. We made a pact that night they we would work even harder next year and make sure we won the flag.

Brad didn't play in the grand final, having been dropped to the second side before the finals. He was less interested in bowling when he found a girlfriend. She was living in Wollongong at the time, so to make the connection happen, he packed up and left Tasmania. Just four months after he arrived, he was off to start his new partnered life.

Daniel had lost total control of his drinking and began to become aggressive. He often broke things in the house and generally locked himself in his room with beer and his television. I stopped buying him alcohol and kept it somewhere he couldn't find it.

By Easter, Daniel was out of control. Even though I wasn't filling the fridge up anymore, he continued to drink excessively. His whole fortnightly Centrelink payment went on bottles of scotch and other alcohol. I didn't know what to do.

The final straw was when he broke two windows in the house and started fighting with friends I had over playing cards. He also threw our platter of nibbles into a wall, making a hole in the plaster and ruining the paint. I rang his grandmother and told him I was kicking him out of the house. If he wasn't gone by Easter Tuesday, I was going to call the police and report him for the damage he had done to the house. He had no money, so his grandmother booked his boat ticket for him.

I stayed with Cameron Tegg for a couple of nights to keep safe. When I returned to the house in Claremont, Daniel and his possessions had disappeared. The windows had not been replaced, the damage to the wall was not fixed, and some of the furniture had also been broken. I had to get the house fixed as soon as possible.

It cost me over $2,000 to fix the damage he had done. It was enough to wipe out most of the money I had left in my bank account. I now had the onus of paying the rent and utilities alone, very little money, and not working. It was time to find a job.

Knowing my favourite job I ever had was night work, I applied for a Night Auditor position at one of Hobart's leading hotels. Working 10:30pm to 7:00am two days a week, it gave me just enough money to survive. I had to ration cigarettes, cut back my drinking, and be careful with the price of groceries I bought.

One winter afternoon I was sitting at home when the power went out. It was a freezing time in Tasmania, and I needed the heater running, so I went to the electricity box to examine the issue. When there, I was confronted by a worker from the electricity company. He said my power would be permanently turned off until both outstanding electricity bills were paid. I was so angry. Both Brad and I had entrusted Daniel with the electricity bill, paying him our one-third share each time he produced the bill. He would then take it to the post office and pay it, or so we thought. He didn't pay the bill at all, just pocketed our money, and left the bill outstanding. I should have at least seen a late payment notice, but these were all sent via email to him. I had no idea the bill hadn't been paid.

It cost me $1,300 to pay the bills and get my power back on. I was now broke, without a dribble of savings to rely on. My fortnightly income was less than my expenses. The stress of my financial situation had a bearing on my ability to work. Even though I only worked 16 hours a week, I often worked under mental duress. I needed the money to try and survive, so I went to work no matter what.

I started to regret my decision to move to Tasmania. I looked after those two boys when they were in a desperate time of their lives, one had left me, and the other had to be sent packing. I was in a diabolical situation. It was either time to move back to Melbourne or try once again to go back to full-time work. I certainly didn't want to head home with my tail between my legs. Knowing my mental health had collapsed every time I attempted to work full-time, it was a risk I had to take to save the situation. I left the hotel to take up a full-time role as an accountant, starting on a graduate wage. It wasn't great money, but a lot more than I was earning at the hotel and would be sure to put me in a steady financial position. All I had to do was stay healthy.

I crossed my fingers.

CHAPTER 37

Nutbush

Pennant started well again at Glenorchy-Rodman (Rodman for short), determined to make amends for the grand final failure from the season before. I wasn't training much due to the long hours of my accounting job. Michael 'Nutbush' Sweeney had joined forces with us, transferring from Rosny Park. He was the enemy just months earlier, but as a great friend of many of our club members, he saw the grass was greener at Rodman and jumped ship.

I burnt out by late November, which was no surprise, and my mental health capitulated to dangerous levels once more. I had no choice but to leave my full-time role and for the umpteenth time, go back on the disability pension. Every time I tried to make something of my life in work, my mental health would let me down. My mind and body weren't up to 40 hours work per week. I'd start off flying high thinking this time would be different, only to get three or four months down the track and be back to square one. This mental collapse resulted in my medication being doubled for over a month, trying to get my mind back to planet earth. I was on the highest dosage allowed to be prescribed, so needed regular visits to the doctor to monitor my recovery.

Under mental stress, I was still selected to skip for Tasmania in the upcoming series against Victoria at Trevallyn. After winning the first test, we drew the second test by getting two shots on the last end, finishing the day undefeated. As Victoria were the current holders of the French-Holbrook shield, we had to win the series to claim it – two wins and a draw each would mean Victoria retained the trophy.

After winning the third test the next morning, we needed just one more victory in the final two tests to achieve an enormous upset. I played the final end of the fourth test against my old skip, Wayne Roberts, with scores tied on the overall board. After my third Aaron Page cleared the way, I was able to get contact on the jack with a reaching backhand shot. We held the series, but Wayne had two bowls left to change that. He missed, I added another shot, and it all came down to Wayne's last bowl. Lying two down on the head, he attempted a weighted shot down his forehand but missed wide, and Tasmania won the series in an enormous boost for the minnow state. It was fair to say that celebrations that evening extended well beyond the curfew time, and many players turned up under the weather for the fifth and final test. We lost the dead rubber but took home the shield. The series win gave us belief that we could push for a medal at the Alley Shield in Canberra next April.

By early December, my lease on the Claremont house was running out and I could move. As I was back on the pension, my income fell below the National thresholds for access to NDIS properties. I ended up scoring a city apartment well under the market value of rent, with car space and easy access to everything in town. Getting my bond back on the Claremont house was made almost impossible by a gestapo real estate agency, seemingly using old photos of the property, wanting me to bring it back to that same condition. The bond refund was critical as I needed it to pay the bond on my new apartment, so I had to put many hours into working on the house.

As I wasn't working, I spent many hours a day sorting out the real estate condition report. It took me a week, but I made the house look far better than it was when the boys moved in. Still, the real estate agent would not return my bond, citing several issues including junk under the house and cobwebs in the gutters. The junk wasn't ours – so I made that point. When it came to the spider webs, I turned nasty on the estate agents. With just two days before I had to move, I wasn't copping any dodgy delay tactics. I remember telling our property manager, "It took 20,000 men and 22 years to build the Taj Mahal and I have no chance of repeating that on Chippendale alone in a couple of days". I think she took my point and decided to sign off on the condition report and release my bond.

I moved into Campbell Street in Hobart just before Christmas. It was a small one-bedroom abode in a brand-new building, but it suited me to the ground. It was modern, easy to clean and low maintenance. It was much easier taking care of an apartment than a three-bedroom house.

I formed a great friendship with Nutbush and also, Rick Ormerod and Deb O'Donnell over the Christmas break. For the first time ever, I didn't visit home in Melton for Christmas. I just didn't have the money to make the trip, nor to buy anyone a present. I spent Christmas day with Josh Tegg and his family in Brighton, making sure I wasn't alone for the occasion. The other days around the festive season were spent having a quiet drink with Nutbush at the Glenorchy RSL or visiting Rick and Deb in Glenorchy. It was the start of a bond that continues to this very day.

Rodman dominated the season and comfortably accounted for Sandy Bay in the grand final at Beltana. It was redemption for the heart-breaking loss just twelve months before and broke a 37-year top grade premiership drought for our Glenorchy-based club. The night is remembered mostly for Nutbush running around gloating that he was the only player to win the flag two years in a row. The more he drank, the more he gloated about it. Anyone who knew the man could only imagine how funny he was rubbing it in.

Reminding us of the year before didn't help with our celebrations but by the time the beer kicked in, we were celebrating Rosny's flag too. Nothing could spoil a history making day for Rodman.

The Alley Shield in Canberra was a solid effort, only losing to New South Wales (NSW), Queensland (QLD), and Victoria (VIC). We finished fourth, one spot higher than the year before. The team honestly believed that we could win a shield before our time together came to an end. It would be all positives moving to Yokine in Perth for the next effort.

I returned to work in April in a hotel for two nights a week as a night auditor. It wasn't the same hotel I had worked at previously, but I knew my body would be able to handle two shifts a week. I was right. I had no mental problems whatsoever coping with the workload. Starting at 11:00pm at night, my shift would run to 7:00am and often involve little face-to-face communication with guests. I was a whizz with the operating system and could generally get through all my necessary work by 2:00am. To make use of the downtime, I began writing. Over the next couple of months, I wrote the first edition of 'In the Zone – Developing Mental Toughness in Lawn Bowls'. The book would be relatively successful, selling over 2,000 e-books through Amazon.

That winter, I found solace playing indoor biased bowls for the first time in almost a decade. It was too cold to play bowls outside and all the grass greens were closed anyway. I led for Cameron Tegg in the State fours, where we were pipped for the gold by Tony Simpson and team in a close round robin competition. I entered the State singles with no expectations, but after moving from my kneeling stance to an upstanding approach, I found some form of old. I went through undefeated in Hobart in the regional division, and again undefeated in the State round robin format to win the Tasmanian State singles. The joy would be short-lived, told I didn't qualify to play for Tasmania at the Nationals because I only played in two State events – go figure? As quick as I started playing indoor bowls again, was as quick as I threw it in. It would be just social pennant for me and no other competitions.

Essendon bowling club contacted me before the next pennant season. They wanted to see if I'd play premier division for them as a fly-in marquee player. Their offer wasn't high, but considering my current income, it was an offer I couldn't refuse. Their schedule allowed me to still play a handful of games for Rodman, meaning I'd qualify for finals in Hobart if we didn't at Essendon. I promised them dedication for one season, but due to inconsistent mental health and the exhaustion of flight travel, it was only ever going to be one year.

My bowls gig at Essendon, my two shifts work at the city hotel, and my part-pension (reduced for income earned) put me in a steady financial position. I felt comfortable financially for the first time in over a year and it helped steady my mental health. I loved my little city apartment and continued strong friendships with bowlers at Rodman. It was the mental release I needed to enjoy life once more.

But there was always a twist.

CHAPTER 38

Court

Centrelink sent me notice that the rules around the Disability Support Pension (DSP) had changed and that my pension was cancelled effective immediately. I could apply for Newstart Allowance and receive a reduced payment for that, but my pension was gone for good.

When doing the maths, I realised these new rules would reduce my income by around $400 per fortnight. I was already on the poverty line, so any reduction in my income would put me in a precarious position. I had to take some sort of action, but through the right Centrelink channels. I appealed the decision and sat waiting patiently for 30 days for a revision of my pension.

If it wasn't for the Essendon payments, I would have been literally on 'the bones of my arse'. So, to make sure I didn't lose my deal there, I trained almost every day in Hobart, hoping that my form would carry to the Melbourne premier division.

I was notified in late October that my appeal against the Centrelink ruling on my DSP was rejected. This left me no other option but to file a case with the Appeals & Administrative Tribunal (AAT). Without money to afford a solicitor, I'd have to fight the case representing myself. I wouldn't get a hearing until the new year, so had plenty of time to assess the new rules and prepare my case. I had studied areas of law at university, but this case was well-above anything I had ever been taught.

Essendon flew into Christmas on top of the premier division ladder, with Melbourne or Clayton the only likely teams to be a force in the finals. I had just won the Moama Prestige Pairs with Mark Nitz, so I had money to afford Christmas at home, as well as gifts for all the family members. I even bought a second-hand Commodore in Hobart, offloading the failing BMW. For Christmas, I bought myself a gift for the first time ever. I contacted Tas Plates and purchased number plates with 'AUS132'. It represented my country and the number of my cap when playing for Australia.

I had a great Christmas at home, making up for my non-attendance the year before. It was so good to see the whole family again after so long, reminding me that they are there if I ever needed them. I was only there four days, but I recall it as my favourite Christmas ever. Everyone seemed so happy to be together and the generosity from everyone with gifts only amplified the love felt amongst our family.

Before pennant started in late January, we had the Tasmanian State championships to play at Buckingham in Hobart. Despite losing the singles semi-final to young Superstar Lachie Sims in a thriller, I was able to snare two State gold medals in the pairs (with Cameron Tegg), and the fours (with Cameron Tegg, Michael Sims, and Robert McMullen). They were my first state titles in Tasmania and provide for great memories today.

My hearing was a disaster at the AAT. Centrelink sent a government lawyer to act on their behalf and he smoked my in the court room. The new rules were complicated and failed to interpret them correctly. It gave the judge no other option but to uphold Centrelink's decision and ratify my ineligibility for the DSP. I was shattered.

The last avenue of appeal I had was to appeal the AAT's decision. I needed to do more research on the rules and get all the necessary paperwork required to try and get my pension back. It wasn't a matter of coming prepared, it was a matter of turning up to the court so organised and prepared, that the judge would take me seriously. With my appeal not taking place until mid-year, I would be stuck in a stalemate for another few months.

Essendon left no stone unturned as we finished on top of the premier division ladder. Two tough finals against Melbourne would bring the best out of our players, as we stormed to the premiership at Mulgrave. It was the first time Essendon had ever won a premier division and it gave me the unusual statistic of having won three premier division flags with three different clubs: Essendon, Bundoora, and Altona.

Tasmania had another fair effort in the Alley Shield. This time we only lost to QLD, NSW, and SA. We had a last round victory against VIC to gain fourth place once again. The side was no longer seen as one of the 'bottom three minnow states', but now a force to be reckoned with.

The trip was soured by poor weather and a personal injury. While on the wet mat against QLD late in a practice match, I slipped. My body went one way and my head the other way. I heard a pop in my neck, and it immediately seized up. I was under intense pain. I couldn't move my head at all, so went straight to the team manager to raise my concerns.

I was taken down to the local physiotherapy centre to have professional hands on my neck. It was a sickening and uncomfortable experience to hear your neck crunching with just the slightest movements and touches. It made me feel light-headed and like I wanted to vomit. In one slight move, I heard a recognisable pop as my neck fell back in place. I was free to move my head again, but still in serious discomfort and pain. I was too scared to move my head at speed or to do any sudden movements whatsoever.

The morning of the opening ceremony, I was back at the physiotherapy receiving final treatment before play. I was offered a heated neck pad to see if it would help with movement and pain. The heat certainly relieved some of my symptoms, so I took it with me to the bowling club. I missed the opening ceremony, but to the relief of the team, I told them I was fit enough to play. Grant Allford was amazing that week, running constantly from the green to the microwave inside, heating up my neck pad. It was a short-term solution to help me get through the four days of play.

The injury didn't fully recover until months later, after numerous visits to a chiropractor and physiotherapist. On colder days, even today, I still get stiffness in my neck.

With the season over, my player payment dried up and finances were on the brink of disaster. I could no longer afford my city apartment and had to move to a run-down unit in West Moonah. Even though it wasn't discounted under the NDIS, it was certainly cheaper. I just had to do it.

My hotel offered me the full-time night auditor position. It was easy to understand why I accepted it. I had lost my DSP and was unlikely to get it back. I was no longer receiving any money for playing bowls and I felt as though I could do it this time. I lost count of how many times I tried to go back to full-time work, but being as stubborn as a mule, I refused to let mental health control my life.

I lasted just five weeks before my mental health crashed once more. I tried to fight on for a few more weeks, but openly crying in front of hotel guests for no reason and having to leave the night desk regularly for fresh air, would eventually lead to my demise. The night manager was a fantastic lady. She did everything she could to help me out, including covering for me for long periods of time while I went outside. She brought me food for dinner to make sure I ate, as well as allowing me to take all the time I needed to complete tasks. Unfortunately for me, the harder I tried to beat the mental issues, the worse I became.

In a meeting with the hotel boss, I came clean about my struggles with anxiety and depression. I was granted a week of compassionate leave and used my three days of annual leave I had accumulated. With ten days off, we were both hopeful that I could recover and come back to work. It wasn't to be, and I resigned a couple of days before my leave expired.

I spent much of the next two weeks with Rick and Deb, staying at their house. I didn't want to be alone with fear of having another nervous breakdown. I slept excessive hours and ate very little, waiting patiently for the mental suffering to go away. To my relief, it started to disappear after a week, and I began to recover. With my court appeal only days away, I had to be fit enough to fight my appeal.

The main trigger for my anxiety and depression was putting my body under duress. I had tried so many times to cope with the responsibility and commitment of full-time work but had failed more times than I could count. I wanted a better life for myself by earning a solid income. I wanted to make something of my life before I got too old. I just wanted to be a normal person who was able to get through a week of work. I wanted to feel like everyone else. I didn't want to rely on government payments. The fact was, I needed the payments to survive, and I had to win the court case. I had to give myself some sort of financial security to ease the money stresses in my life.

When I attended the court, I noticed the same judge was sitting for the appeal. I immediately lost confidence. It was a slow start from my end, but my life was on the line and determination kicked in. I produced every single document the judge wanted to see. The government lawyer attempted to discredit what I tabled, questioning the qualifications of my psychologist and the details of the reports. It was a long hearing and a fight I was not willing to stand down from. This was my final chance to get the pension back, or I would forever be under financial pressure.

After two hours of hammer and tong, the government lawyer showed his authority by asking the judge to dismiss my appeal so he could get to more important things. I couldn't believe that a guy on $1,000 an hour could be so arrogant and inconsiderate about my long-running battle with poor mental health. He was brazening enough to highlight that anyone with a mental disability shouldn't be able to be so organised and capable of representing themselves in a court of appeal. The bastard. I wasn't an idiot. I wasn't dumb. What I was, was sick, and I needed government income support to live.

I held my emotions in check and refused to verbally attack my opponent. My focus was on answering the judge's questions and giving her every piece of paper she asked for. I stayed calm under pressure, despite sweating profusely, and continued to fight for my life.

When handing down her decision, the judge said that I had satisfied the four main requirements of an application for the DSP. She upheld my appeal and ordered Centrelink to put me on the pension effective immediately, as well as back-pay me the difference between Newstart Allowance and the DSP, from the date I applied almost 12 months earlier – including interest! The government lawyer was disgusted. As he threw his papers in his carry bag, he turned to me and said, "You won? Happy?" and stormed out of the tribunal.

I sat there for a few moments as the judge was neatly putting her paperwork into a pile. I was overwhelmed with emotion and began to sob in the chair. She looked up, showing concern, but not saying a word. As I stood up, I turned to her and said, "Thank you. You might have just saved a life," and left.

I beat Centrelink in court representing myself.

Without doubt, the victory in court gave me a new lease on life. I had enough money to meet all general expenses, including operating a motor vehicle. Things were tight at times, but if I lived with my means, I could survive comfortably.

Only days passed before Rosny Park contacted me about playing for them and taking on the club coaching role in 2016/17. Not working, the eight hours per week coaching was within the rules of my pension, and if payment was spread out across a twelve-month period, I wouldn't lose a cent of my Centrelink payment. The deal was also under the first tax bracket, and with my pension being tax-free, I wouldn't have any income tax liability. It was the most money I could possibly earn without being taxed or reduced to a part-pension.

I knew my health would cope fine with the weekly hours. Enjoying bowls so much, it would be a more pleasurable experience to help club members, than feeling like work. My hours were flexible and my requirements dependent on members wanting to be coached. It was a perfect opportunity for me.

It was an offer I couldn't resist.

CHAPTER 39

Heart

Rosny Park was one of the biggest clubs in Hobart. It had three grass greens, an enormous clubhouse, and about six pennant sides. It was a club with a proud history, boasting Tasmania's only every male player to win the Australian Champion of Champions singles, the late Ron Brooks. The club had local legends John Boatwright and Mick Eiszelle, as well as club stalwarts David Genford, Patrick Hoffman, and Darren Monks. They had a solid top side and were a chance of winning the premiership.

Nutbush and Rick made the move to Rosny Park with me. Our friendship had blossomed and the thought of playing together in the same rink, was something we all wanted to happen. My coaching contract was designed to help the club take the next step across all divisions. Being an ageing club, it was always going to be a tough ask.

I'd get the rink I wanted for pennant, but it proved to be too strong in the context of the side. We would continually win comfortably on our rink but continued to battle overall. We won many close matches before the selectors decided to take Nutbush out of our four and skip him in another rink. He would be replaced by Patrick Hoffman.

I went back to the Victorian Open for a second time and came home with a gold medal in the pairs with newly befriended Bradley Marron and claimed the silver once again in the singles. This time around, I was wiped off the Shepparton indoor carpet by Victorian State skipper, Matt Flapper. The extended schedule meant I played over more days than previously, so I thought I'd have another go at it.

By Christmas, we were second on the ladder and playing decent bowls. I'd won the club singles, pairs, triples, and fours in my first year, and went into the break confident in myself, as well as the team.

2017 dawned, and little did I know at the time, it would be a year of my life I would never, ever forget. Rosny Park flew home in pennant to finish on top of the ladder and earn a home double-chance semi-final against Kingborough. I won the Hobart region Champion of Champions singles and advanced to the final three in the State. Tasmania picked me for the fourth consecutive year in a row to skip the State team, this time alongside Robert 'Rowdy' McMullen, Andrew Whitmore, and Scott Summers.

After beating the Kingborough Tigers on an 18 second Rosny track, we advanced to the grand final at Howrah. In a rematch against the Tigers, they handled the slow and tracky surface far better than we did, leaving us to ponder what could have been. I might have played in a solid rink win against Tony Clarke, but it was nowhere near enough to cover the smashing we copped across the green. We just weren't the best side on the day, simple.

I played the State Champion of Champions singles finals at Kings Meadows in Launceston. The deciding match ended up between me and my great mate and State third, Rowdy. We had been into many battles together in the past and had never played against each other. Rowdy shot off out of the gates and led me 13-3, but I turned the match around and ran away with the State title 21-16. It was my fifth State Champion of Champions singles, and I was now just two behind Bosisto.

The following two days I teamed up with Michael 'Nutbush' Sweeney and Grant 'Bag' Allford in the State triples championships held at the same venue. We won through our section with no issues on day one and had even bigger wins in our quarter final and semi-final on day two. We faced Jason Little, Josh Appleyard, and Tim Douce in the State final, with 18 ends to decide a winner.

The match had many dead ends and went well past our expected finishing time. It was close all the way, and we led by just four shots with two ends to play. Nutbush and Bag had a shocker penultimate end and with just one bowl remaining, I lay four or five shots down at the head. After dropping short with my first effort, I had to make sure my final shot was given a chance. To my team's delight, I trailed the jack for two shots, and we entered the last end six in front. We hung on to win the match by five and score my second gold medal in three days. It was also my fourth Tasmanian State title, to go alongside the ten I had won in Victoria. I was building a decent resume and started to rate my chances of being selected in the Australian squad again, after a six-year absence.

The trip to Adelaide for the 2017 Alley Shield would be more famous for a Tasmanian silver medal, than it would be for a South Australian gold medal. We won five of our first six games, only losing a thriller to South Australia by just two shots. Among our wins were massive margins over NSW, WA, and a double-digit win over QLD.

Going into the final day of competition, we held top spot in front of SA by two rink wins. We both had five wins, and our scoring margin was supreme, so a final round win against VIC with even one rink up, would secure Tasmania's first Alley shield.

Halfway through the match, we led the Big V by a single shot. Michael Sims was 23 shots in front of Barrie Lester's rink, Mark Nitz was 15 behind Aaron Wilson's team, and my boys were battling hard to be seven behind Matt Flapper. Our manager was notified by a Bowls Australia scorer that Tasmania had been docked a rink due to a scoring error against the ACT, who we beat in round one. Whether it was our fault for not picking up on it, or the scorers for making the mistake, or both parties, it didn't hide the fact that we were now only one rink in front of SA.

News filtered across the greens that SA were cleaning up the ACT on all three rinks. They weren't going to catch our margin, but a win on three rinks for them meant that we needed two rinks to stay in front. With Nitz in all sorts of trouble, and Sims guaranteeing us one rink win, it was obvious that my rink had to get the other point.

Sims finished 19 in front, while Nitz hung tough to lose by 14. My rink played the last end tied with Flapper at 18-18. SA had already finished and got maximum points in their match, so it all came down to my rink's last end. Victoria needed a five to draw the test and six to beat us, while all we needed was the last end to take home the gold.

The Victorians killed the last end no fewer than seven times, as my boys played their absolute guts out. It was the eighth replay of the final end that decided our destiny. Lying two down on the head, I swung forehand at the jack in an attempt put it in the ditch. Watching the bowl go down the green I knew it was close. I got the jack dead-centre and it headed to the ditch with my bowl right behind it, possibly making it unbeatable.

In a moment of heartbreak, the jack reached the ditch and instead of sitting in the sand, it bobbled out to three Victorian bowls near the boundary line. I ripped off my hat and threw it on the ground in disgust. Surely, we couldn't be robbed an elusive Alley Shield because of bad luck. Flapper attempted to add a fourth shot but left his bowl out of bounds. I hadn't had a draw shot in an hour but did have two and a half-feet of room for the shot. Although Flapper had a bowl left, he would need to attempt the kill instead of my bowl, as he was chasing a minimum of five.

I released my bowl confident in the line I took, but unsure if I was reaching. A slight cross wind pushed my bowl wide of its line and despairingly, it didn't track back in bounds. The Alley Shield was gone if Flapper didn't kill the end. He chose to drive at two of our bowls away from the jack that would make five shots for them but missed. Tasmania won the match, but my rink had lost, and we had also lost the shield.

I had never cried after a game of bowls before. Even when we received our silver medals to a standing ovation from the other teams and crowds, I couldn't help but be upset and disappointed. I always say that it would have been the greatest thing to ever happen to men's bowls in Australia, if Tasmania had of won that shield.

The silver medal left a bitter taste in my mouth for many reasons. I had the chance to win it for the State and failed. I had to look all my teammates in the eyes and apologise for the loss. I had to be somewhat content with a tenth Alley Shield silver medal, never having won a gold.

Today in Tasmania, the final match of the Adelaide Alley Shield is taboo. Anyone who raises conversation about the jack bouncing out of the ditch is generally ignored and dissed. Others who talk about it can be verbally abused or attacked for ever mentioning it. Some of the players from that match would never set foot in Tasmanian colours again. They honestly believed that it was our time and the failure to win it was so devastating, they could never try again. The State hasn't looked like winning the Alley shield since, and it would take a huge turnaround of recent form to ever look like winning it. Maybe Adelaide was the chance for Tasmania to reign supreme, but it wasn't meant to be. A sad twist of fate would be the only difference between being champions or losers.

It still hurts today.

CHAPTER 40

Swine

Brad Griffiths came back to live with me in Moonah in May 2017, while his girlfriend and son stayed in Melbourne with family. They were looking for a place to call their own, but due to lack of space where they stayed, Brad moved back in with me for a few months.

I had just started working in a bookkeeping firm in Howrah, doing 15 hours per week over three days. I was healthily managing the job while not coaching in the off-season and found bookkeeping work to be comfortable and rewarding. The role started my interest in Goods and Services Tax (GST) and the applications of it to businesses and individuals.

I also agreed to a fly-in contract as a marquee player for Ashfield bowling club in Sydney. It was our bowling off-season, so I had plenty of time to spare on the weekends.

The Australian squad came out in early July and once again I wasn't part of it. The only way I would be likely to see green and gold on my back again was to win the upcoming Australian Champion of Champions singles in Darwin. By winning that, I would earn Australia's place for the World Champion of Champions singles and have the opportunity of winning a world level medal. It became a priority for me to get back in those colours. If this was my only way to get there, I simply had to do it.

After a Chinese take-away meal on a cold July evening, I fell grossly ill. During the night, I got up multiple times to vomit in the sink. I spewed until there was nothing left to throw-up. Even when my stomach was empty, the pain and cramps forced me to dry reach, making it difficult to sneak a breath in. I was trying to take in some water, but it just came back up within seconds. Brad too was feeling unwell but had nothing on the symptoms I was experiencing.

By 6:00am I couldn't stand it any longer. Brad had nursing experience and suggested we call an ambulance. I sat there waiting for almost an hour before the paramedics arrived. Obviously exhausted from being sick, I had lost all colour in my face and didn't even have the energy to stand up.

I never had faith in the Tasmanian Health system at the time and this was no different. After checking my vital signs and asking me a couple of questions, the paramedics did nothing more than suggest fluids and rest, and a visit to my doctor that day. I was in agony with stomach pains and not able to even keep a mouthful of water in my stomach, yet they left without concern.

At 8:00am when my doctor opened, I called to make an urgent appointment. Brad drove my car to the doctors as I had no chance of even looking up, let alone driving a motor vehicle. Without delay I was rushed into the surgery and assessed on the bed. My doctor couldn't even place a finger on my stomach without me screaming in pain. Her level of concern was far higher than the paramedics and she ordered me straight to hospital. She filled out a document to take with me so that I'd avoid triage and be taken straight through.

On arriving at the emergency room, I was put in a wheelchair and run down the hall by two nurses. They put a canula in my wrist and started bag fluids immediately. Somewhere between the doctors and hospital I had soiled myself from both ends and had to send Brad home to get me some clean clothes.

Along with blood tests and a sample of my faeces from my soiled underwear, the doctors were able to quickly identify that I had salmonella food poisoning. My reaction and symptoms were severe, so I was put on antibiotics immediately and placed on 'nil by mouth'. The morphine they gave me eased the excruciating stomach pains and allowed me to sleep.

It took four days in hospital before I was clear to leave. I had the option to lodge a complaint against the paramedics, but I refused to do so, saying their job was far too important to be dealing with paperwork. Brad picked me up and we immediately went home to give the house a deep clean. We scrubbed every corner of the house, making sure it was spotless. My immune system was weak after the food poisoning and any infection in the near future could cause complications to my health.

It was late-July when I again fell sick. This time, my mental health went rock-bottom. I doubled up on my medication and was prescribed Valium to help relax. I developed excessive shaking, Parkinson's-like, and was prescribed further pills to help with that.

I visited the hospital emergency department twice that week, but merely sent home every time with extra medication. My cocktail of drugs had done nothing to improve my health; in fact, I got severely worse.

Ashfield had qualified for the State Pennant finals in early August, and I had ambitions of flying up there to compete. I waited right until the evening before I was due to fly before calling them and withdrawing. I was far too sick to be travelling. I had more important issues to deal with than a State pennant.

I lost my co-ordination and began hallucinating at home. I saw animals in my living room clear as a bell, remembering specifically the vivid colours of a toucan and the prominent stripes of a zebra.

Near my door was a perfectly rectangular image of a playing card, the ace of spades. My weight plummeted and just a week into my new battle, I had already lost twelve kilograms.

Brad found me taking extra Valium pills and hid the bottle from me. They were addictive and sent me to sleep, so every time I woke up, I wanted one. I wasn't in pain when I was asleep, nor did I have to deal with the overwhelming anxiety.

Brad Marron made his way over from Melbourne, concerned that I was suffering a life-threatening illness. He was there to provide any support I required in conjunction with Brad Griffiths. Considering I was asleep 20 hours a day, their main jobs were to ensure I took my correct dosage of medications and to make sure they were always hidden from me, so I didn't overdose.

My next trip to the doctor was concerning. My blood tests had come back negative for everything they had tested for, my weight-loss was as astounding as it was dangerous, and my shaking and tremor was out of control. It was likely I had over-dosed on my anti-depressants some days earlier and I developed serotonin syndrome. My mental state was diabolical, and my body was failing me.

On my third visit to the emergency department, I was hospitalised with serotonin syndrome and placed on fluids. I had numerous blood tests done over the next couple of days, trying to figure out why I was so sick. Despite endless bags of fluids, my weight had continued to drop heavily and the doctor's showed grave concerns. My vital signs were weak, and I wasn't reacting well to any medication orally or through the drip. They were completely stumped and unable to work out what was wrong with me. A nurse had even asked me if I was religious and would like a priest to visit the ward.

Almost 20 kilograms lighter and on death's door, I finally got an answer. My symptoms were so severe that the doctors had never thought to test for Swine flu. It had been eight years since the Swine flu pandemic hit Australia and most people with the illness recovered in a few days with no complications. Doctors thought that I may have had underlying conditions which led to the amplified symptoms, so had to run tests for HIV, among other things. I had asthma which could possibly make it worse, but nowhere near that level.

I was given medication to help with my condition and my recovery began almost straight away. Whatever went through my drip was a wonder drug. Within two days I was back to normal physical health and given the all-clear to go home.

My immune system was suffering from a shocking case of salmonella just a fortnight before, so the doctors determined that this amplified my viral infection. I was warned to keep a close eye on my health as two severe illnesses in a such a short period could send me into shock, or worse still, result in a meltdown mentally.

I had to slow down immediately, get rest, and look after myself. Unfortunately, my mental situation had already collapsed, and I was on the verge of a nervous breakdown.

I was selected to play for the Australian Professional Bowls Association (PBA) side to play against New Zealand at Deer Park in a week's time. I had already booked the flights, planning on visiting my family for two days beforehand. The likelihood of me playing was next to zero, and those were better odds than me even getting on the plane.

Three days before I left, I woke in the morning covered in sweat, anxious and my heartbeat was racing. I popped Valium that I found in Bradleigh's luggage and double medication, trying to stop the onset of an anxiety attack. While taking my tablets, I collapsed in the kitchen and hit my head on the cupboards. Both Brad's were out, so I must have been unconscious for some time. When I woke, my anxiety had completely overwhelmed me. I wanted to stand up to try and walk it off, but my legs were too weak. All I could do was crawl across the floor to my bed and sit up against it. I didn't even have the energy to lift myself onto the mattress.

When the Brad's got home, I'd fallen asleep against my bed. They saw I had found the Valium and were obviously concerned. Neither of them woke me, but they did sit down and wait for me to wake up. Bradleigh was angry I had gone through his luggage to find the pills and had already hidden them again. I knew I was mentally 'gone' and didn't even apologise. My mind was fried, and I didn't want to be conscious.

The only clear thoughts I had were what I had been through the last time I had a nervous breakdown. There was no chance I would fight through that again. My immune system was down, my mind completely out of control, and the mixture of drugs in my body were only fighting each other. I started resigning to life. I didn't want to be alive anymore. I didn't want to suffer anymore.

Marron had a flight booked to Melbourne the same day as mine, but his plane was earlier than mine. I planned to use every last iota of strength I had to make sure I got on that plane. I wasn't going to Melbourne to play the PBA; I didn't even pack my bowls shoes. I was going to make the trip to make sure I was with family. I regret not seeking help from Mum and Dad when I went through my last nervous breakdown. But this one was different. I didn't want to even try and fight it. I had no fight left in me. My survival instinct was gone.

I was going home to die.

When at Hobart airport, I had a massive attack of anxiety and had to call Mum. She talked to me all the way up until I boarded. She did everything possible to calm me down and make sure I got on that plane. She wanted her eldest son in her company so she could try and help me. Although calm in her voice, I knew she was suffering on the inside. Seeing one of your children as sick as I was must have been eating at her heart. All she wanted to do was hug me and tell me everything was going to be okay.

When the plane took off, I was sure it would be the last time I saw Tasmania. Griffiths stayed behind to look after my apartment, but I didn't plan on returning. To distract myself from thinking on the plane, I pulled out my laptop and wrote my final will and testament. With barely any assets to my name, I wasn't leaving much behind, but didn't want to burden anyone once I had gone.

Marron met me at the airport and made sure I got to Mum's safely. When home, I couldn't help but notice the distress in Mum's eyes. I must have been a sight for sore eyes, under-weight, pale, shaking, and a shadow of my former self. I can't imagine what was going through her mind, but as mothers do, she immediately acted.

Before I had unpacked my luggage, she asked to see every pill and tablet I was on. She pushed my anti-depressants aside which I had been on for many years and piled up everything else I had been taking. She opened them all and tipped them in the sink, flushing them down the drain. Mother knew best, and the only way I could begin to recover was to get off the mixture of medications. She only allowed me my single anti-depressant every morning, and nothing else.

Mum set up my old room and allowed me to unpack. I was exhausted from the flight and ended up taking a nap, only to be woken by Mum telling me I had to get out of bed and wait until night to sleep.

The next 18 days of my life were nothing short of unbearable.

From the second night at home, I heard clear voices in my head. They scared me to the point of tears. They were so cruel, so painful, so wrong, and so dangerous. The voices were telling me to stop Mum from helping me by hurting her. They were telling me I had to kill her. I constantly punched myself in the head trying to stop them. They were so real.

I wanted to kill myself that night. With me gone, there was no way my Mum could be harmed. I would be free from mental distress and my family could get on with their lives safely. Knowing I was out of control, I felt obligated to tell Mum about the voices. At first startled, she tried to put me at ease. She knew I wouldn't hurt her no matter what the voices were telling me. I knew I had scared the living daylights out of her. I went to bed in tears, wishing there was a lock on the door from the outside so that I couldn't get out.

Mum and Dad had recently separated, and Dad was living with Nan. Mum called Dad and confronted him with what I had told her. He immediately made his way over to the house and ensured Mum was protected from me. He would spend much of the next two weeks at home doing everything he could to also help me.

The first time Dad saw me, he was speechless. He had never seen me so sick before. He didn't understand why I would just sit on the couch all day watching television and occasionally just burst into tears for no apparent reason. I'm sure that seeing his son in such a state, and being unable to cure me, must have been hard for him. He was a man. Men like to solve problems. This wasn't a problem that could be solved, and that was frustrating for him.

Dad wasn't one to get scared. The only time I ever saw the look of fear in his eyes was when we dealt with the ghosts of Laverton in the early 1990's, when the whites of his eyes were bright like high beam lights in a car. This was the second time I saw that look in his eyes. He was petrified of me and what I had become, but he wouldn't dare leave me alone with Mum. He would stay as long as he had to.

I used the services of Lifeline Australia every night. I'd open the chat and type my concerns to a counsellor. I had to tell them exactly how I was feeling and what I was thinking. I didn't want to talk verbally, so the chat option was convenient for me. My main concern was not for me, but for my Mum. I wanted to stop the thoughts of harming her. If I couldn't stop those thoughts, I was willing to take my own life.

Lifeline Australia were a life saver. I was constantly reminded that these thoughts were just that, only thoughts. Everyone gets bad thoughts from time to time, but it doesn't mean we act on them.

Even if we aren't in control of the thoughts in our head, we can still control the actions we take. It didn't matter what the mind was telling us to do, it mattered how we acted on those thoughts.

That advice gave me my first positive vibes in weeks. I learnt that even if my head was telling me to do horrible things, I didn't have to act on it. I could just talk out aloud to myself, dismissing the thoughts and saying things such as, "Good one voices", or "Not today mate". I couldn't control what I was thinking, but I could tell the thoughts that I wasn't going to act on them. I was in charge of the actions I took, and I wasn't willing to act on anything unless it was positive.

Over the next week I learnt to dismiss awful thoughts and act on positive ones. If I felt hungry, I would eat. If I was thirsty, I would drink. If I felt like a walk, I would go. If I felt like laughing, I would. But if anything crossed my mind that was toxic, I'd dismiss it out aloud. Sometimes I'd be sitting in the living room alone, or with Mum, and just blurt out a dismissal of negative thoughts. It was my way of learning to take control of my own mind. It may have appeared though I was talking to myself, but Mum knew exactly what I was doing.

I truly believed now that I could recover. My suicidal thoughts had gone. The thoughts or harming my Mum had been dismissed so many times, that even they started to go. I regained my appetite and was able to enjoy the pleasure of homecooked meals.

By the end of the second week, I knew I was getting better. My weight had stabilised, even though I was grossly thin. I was eating well and keeping my fluids up. The colour in my face had started to return. I was in no way cured but had become more comfortable dealing with anxiety and depression. I knew the illness would never go away entirely, but I could learn how to live with it. I could make decisions based on my thoughts and dismiss any thought that was negative. I had power again. I had control. I felt like I owned me again.

I returned to Tasmania toward the end of August, weak but happy. I had discovered the way to deal with my mental illness. Of course, I'd get bad days from time to time, but I could deal with bad days. What I wanted was to stop the bad days turning into bad weeks and bad months. If I could get six good days a week out of seven, then to me, life was worth living. It was a modest, yet achievable goal.

I survived a second nervous breakdown.

If mental illness taught me anything, it was that no matter how much it hurt and how tough it got, things would eventually get better. Mental illness is purely thoughts. Thoughts are not actions. You decide your actions. You decide how you react to your thoughts. It doesn't own you. You have a choice. Make the right decisions and you can learn to live with mental illness.

What an extraordinary epiphany!

CHAPTER 41

Impossible

I hadn't had any alcohol for a month and decided to stay off it completely. I thought that if I didn't drink, the likelihood of a relapse would be significantly lowered.

September came and I was able to fulfill my pre-season coaching duties with Rosny Park. Although weak and often exhausted, I tried to put responsibility back in my life. I had returned to work as a bookkeeper and things started to look on the up again. Life was returning to normal, slowly but surely.

By early October, I started training for the Australian Champion of Champions singles in Darwin. I couldn't train for very long each time, but the effort was there. I may have been rolling up on slow grass greens in the cool Tasmanian Spring, completely opposite to the conditions expected in Darwin, but the sessions helped improve my endurance. To get through seven matches of singles in the NT heat, I had to be as fit as possible before I left. Despite all the training I put in, I was still entering the tournament under-prepared, low on confidence, and still frail.

The heat hit me like a bullet when I landed in Darwin. It wasn't the numbers on the temperature gauge that hurt the most, it was the extreme humidity. Wet season had begun a little earlier than expected and the humidity was off the charts. The synthetic green for the championships was running about 18 seconds, well above the 11 second tracks I had trained on, and it was unbearably hot under the covered green. I only managed to train for about an hour on the practice day before the heat affected me. Getting through the seven games was going to be a battle, especially considering the quality of finalists in the field.

In round one, I had a 21-15 win over Breeze Howard from the ACT. My next game was against Jono Davis from NSW, and he cleaned me up 21-12. My third and final game of day one was a disaster. I was suffering from the heat and barely had the energy to get from one end of the green to the other. I played rash shots away from my game plan, realising I had to win in an hour, or I would have no chance after that. Thankfully the game only lasted an hour, but not to my benefit. Clive Adams from WA turned on a singles masterclass and slaughtered me 21-7. My shot at the gold medal was gone, sitting second last on the table.

Suffering heat stroke and dehydration (despite drinking many litres of water), I returned to the hotel to stand under the cold shower. My whole chest had exploded in heat rash and the shock of the cold water made me light-headed and dizzy. Sitting at the end of day one with a single win and a margin of minus 17, I needed to someone to talk to.

I made a few phone calls, telling my mates how much I was suffering in Darwin. I was disappointed with my results and shattered that I wouldn't be able to win the title and take Australia's place at the world championships. All my friends refused to offer sympathy. They reminded me that even competing just weeks after food poisoning, swine flu, and a nervous breakdown, was an achievement in itself. They encouraged me to be kind to myself, remembering that the harsh conditions were never going to make my shot at the title easy.

Heading out for something to eat, I decided to have a beer. I stopped at the local pub, ordered some food, and sat down with an ice-cold froffie. It tasted so good. I had forgotten how good a beer was on a hot day and it made me smile. So, I had another, and another. Tipsy, I left the pub late evening and stumbled back to my room. I decided that my final four matches in the championships would be a celebration of being there, and not to put any pressure on myself. It was the lift I needed.

The second morning, I had a win against local Trystan Smallacombe 21-11 and climbed a spot on the table. In the afternoon I trailed Australian player Wayne Ruediger from SA 0-8, before a run of 21-2 gave me an eleven-shot victory 21-10. With two games left on the final day, I had climbed into contention for the bronze medal and had a sneaky chance at silver. Both Barrie Lester from VIC and Clive Adams from WA had four wins and a solid margin, so one of them would likely win the gold medal.

On the final morning, I shot out to a 19-2 lead against Kurt Brown from QLD and looked like I could get my margin up with Barrie's and Clive's. Kurt made a decent comeback and reduced my final margin to 10 shots, in what appeared to ruin any chance I had of a gold or silver medal. To my shock, Barrie lost to Breeze Howard, opening a chance for the silver medal. The gold was surely Clive's.

I had Barrie in the final round, so a win would guarantee me a silver medal. Should I win, and Clive lose to Trystan, I could snatch the gold medal. If I lost against Barrie, I would tumble down the leaderboard and miss the medals completely.

After almost two hours of play, Trystan had got over the line against Clive Adams, relegating him to the bronze medal. Jono Davis had also won his last game, guaranteeing him the silver medal. The winner of my game with Barrie would take gold, while the loser would finish fifth. I was up 17-11 at the time and began to feel nervous, accompanied by a string of negative thoughts that started to enter my head.

As with my nervous breakdown, I chose to dismiss the negative thoughts and put all my focus into each bowl I had to play. I would gratefully accept any positive thoughts that entered my mind but would not let them distract me from my game plan. I needed just four to win.

At 20-13 I held match and Barrie played a super shot to try and save the game. He trailed the jack off my close bowl, but unfortunately for him, it rolled too far and my bowl behind the head became the match-winner. With five wins and a margin of +22, I became the newest Australian champion. The gold medal was mine and I had the ticket to the 2018 World Champion of Champions singles in Sydney. After eight long years, I could finally put on that green and gold uniform I so desperately craved.

Some say that coming back to win the gold medal after day one was the biggest miracle they have witnessed. Not to me. The biggest miracle I ever witnessed was getting through my health battles that most recent winter. Surviving that, starting the tournament as I did, and going on to win the title, is all a miracle in itself. But without what mental illness had taught me, I would have likely crumbled under pressure in the final match and lost. It should have been impossible for me to win it. I shouldn't have been a realistic chance. Nothing was in my favour going into the tournament and not one person in their right mind would have backed me.

Good things really do come to those who deserve them.

CHAPTER 42

Road

I had another great run at the Victorian Open in November, winning gold in the triples and mixed pairs, and for the third straight time in the event, a silver in the singles. Mitch Sidebottom from South Bendigo was too good in the final, jumping out of the gates and hanging on for a hard-earned gold medal. Thankfully, my consistent tournament and three medals paid dividends when I won the 'Vic Medal' for best player in the tournament. It was pleasing to win an award that was initially brought in because of my 'marathon man' efforts of 2012.

Everything about my bowls for the next twelve months was all directed to the World championship. I had never trained so hard, nor put in so much work on my mental approach.

Brad and I moved to a big house in Moonah to housesit for a friend, while his partner and child flew down to Hobart to join us.

I lived downstairs where I had my own area, while Brad and his family took the upstairs area.

Every Tuesday was the boys' night out. We would venture down to the Valern in Moonah, drink schooners of XXXX Gold and have a social hit on our favourite machine. We would generally always lose but spending the night with 'Jorje' and 'Hennifer', as we called two of the symbols on the screen, never got old.

The win in Darwin gave me the belief that I could conquer the world. Pennant was going well once again and I'd won the club singles, pairs, and fours. My health was almost perfect, and all the stars were aligning for a World singles title.

After Christmas I'd finally win my first Tasmanian singles championship, and although running deep into the draw of the fours and pairs, I didn't win any medals in those events. I also won the State Champion of Champions singles, my sixth State win in that event, making it back-to-back. Add this to a last bowl miracle in the State triples final to make four shots, and it was three State titles in one year. It also earnt me Tasmanian Bowler of the year for the second time.

Rosny dominated the second half of the pennant season but failed again in the grand final. This time it was my old club Rodman who cleaned us up at Sandy Bay. My rink had a good win against Tony Vince, but it just wasn't enough. It was the second year in a row that my rink fought their backsides off, only to see other rinks torn apart in a devastating loss.

The second consecutive grand final loss made me question my effectiveness as coach of Rosny. My contract was up for renewal, and I had a meeting set after Easter. The meeting never eventuated as I bit the bullet and resigned in my role, stating that if I couldn't coach the team we currently had to a premiership, I had no hope of doing it in the future. My plan was to stay on at Rosny as a bowler, enjoy my 15 hours per week as a bookkeeper, and potentially look for a marquee player fly-in role in Melbourne.

The owners had by now returned to their property and Brad and his family moved back to the mainland. I found a little apartment in West Moonah thanks to help from Nutbush and the local real estate, giving me the perfect little place to live.

My plans came to fruition as I all but signed on at Deer Park as a marquee player, before finding out the intricacies of the deal. Their offer was very reasonable from a financial viewpoint, but after finding out I'd need to cover my own plane trips and airport transfers, the deal lost its appeal. For those reasons, I turned it down and the deal fell through.

The same day I knocked back the marquee offer, I was contacted by Brad Marron about playing and coaching for Bendigo East. The club didn't muck around. The very next day I had an email in my inbox with an offer from Bendigo East. The proposal was to fly over on a Thursday morning, coach the sides on Thursday afternoon, run a club bistro on Friday night, and play pennant for the club on Saturday. I'd then fly home on the 6:00am plane to Hobart on Sunday mornings to be available for regional events and club championships with Rosny.

With my health flying and Brad Griffiths gone, I decided to take the job on.

The news spread like wildfire through social media and there was a buzz in the Bendigo area. My Tasmanian friends and colleagues weren't at all disappointed because I wasn't going there permanently. I was still a Rosny member and planning to continue playing for Tasmania in State representative bowls.

Whether it was the announcement, or my recent wins on the bowling green, or maybe a mixture of both, I made the Australian emerging squad, the tier below the main open squad. Many years I sat back with disappointment each time the squads were announced. This was my ticket back into the environment and I didn't want to let it slip.

Grant Allford spent wintery mornings at Glenorchy City with me completing drills and activities required by the Australian coaches. I didn't just do the drills for the hell of it, I did them under match-like conditions. Not only that, but I also did way more drill cards than I was ever required to do. With the World's only a few months away, I used the exercises as not only to tick the boxes for Australian selectors, but to best prepare myself for a shot at a world title. Many of those mornings were sub zero temperatures with ice covering the outdoor carpet green. Even if I had to wear four layers of clothing, beanie, and earmuffs, I wasn't going to miss a single training session.

Just before my season kicked off in Bendigo, the finals of the Australian Champion of Champions singles were held. After the horrific temperatures and conditions in Darwin, I would be put to the test in a whole new environment. The championships were at Kingborough, thirty minutes south of Hobart. Earlier that year I won the regional and State legs of the event at the same club; and now I had the opportunity to win the National title there too.

For three days, the temperature never passed 12 degrees. Being early in the season, the greens were between 11 and 12 seconds, considered very slow and heavy to the mainlanders.

On day one I had hard fought wins against Wayne Ruediger from SA, Warren Holt from WA, and Mark Malgorski from the NT. Along with Wayne, Barrie Lester, was also back for the second consecutive year after both winning their own State Champion of Champions singles back-to-back.

The second day came, and I had two thrilling wins against David Ferguson from NSW by a single shot, and Ryan Bester from QLD by just two.

By the third morning, only Barrie or myself could win the gold. After I had a quick win against Mac Maclean from the ACT, I sat and watched Barrie escape a tight match against Wayne Ruediger. It meant that our final round match, like in Darwin, would decide the gold medal. Circumstances were a little different though, as this time the loser was guaranteed silver.

On the streamed rink, I got off to a flyer through solid draw bowls and accurate hitting. Even a slight bit of nerves toward the end of the match didn't stop me as I ran away with a 21-12 win and the gold medal – for the second time in as many years.

For someone to win an Australian Champion of Champions singles, they have to win their club singles title, regional singles title, State singles title, and then win the round robin format at the Australian finals. Not only had I done that two years in a row, but I'd also done it in polar opposite conditions. To win on an 18 second synthetic in the unbearable heat of Darwin, and then win on heavy greens in the freezing, windy conditions of a Tasmanian spring, certainly made me realise that I wasn't a one-trick pony. I also had the uncanny situation of qualifying for the 2019 World Champion of Champions singles before I had even played the 2018 event!

With two opportunities to play in the green and gold ahead, as well as participating in the Australian emerging squad program, it seemed my career was back on track to do something special.

Better late than never.

CHAPTER 43

World

My trips to Bendigo were very enjoyable. I'd get to spend time with a great mate, coach bowlers of all different levels, fulfill one of my favoured hobbies, cooking, and play on the best greens in Australia.

Bendigo is a long way from Moonah, but I used the travel times as rest and recuperation. It generally took me seven hours from door to door, so there was a lot of downtime to take it easy.

The bistro became an immediate success at the club, making them hundreds of dollars each Friday night. The increased bar and raffle sales also yielded good results, virtually paying for my contract by itself. The training nights on Thursdays had no spare rinks whatsoever, with the club getting behind their new coach. Pennant was also a raging success, seeing the mighty Magpies destroy quality teams across the pennant competition.

Late in October I headed up to Sydney to compete in the World Champion of Champions singles at St Johns Park. Our accommodation was half an hour away from the venue, so it was crucial not to miss the bus. The schedule was also difficult with a one game on, one game off format. It was also sets play, which I despised, being two sets of nine ends and a three-end tie-breaker if necessary. Even against minnow countries, you were expected to play out every match in the qualification rounds.

The greens were upward of 18 seconds and many of the newly established bowling countries could not handle the pace of the surface. It was evident that most of the field were not in medal contention, but they had won their National title and deserved their place in the field.

My draw appeared tricky, with tough matches against Scotland, Wales, South Africa, Malaysia, and the United States. My other matches were against Spain, Norfolk Island, Samoa, Macau, Switzerland, Zimbabwe, Botswana, and Hungary.

Pulling on the green and gold for my first game against Scotland was simply incredible. I had full body tingles the second the shirt went over my head. I had this overwhelming sense of pride and satisfaction wearing the uniform. It had been seven and a half years since I had the pleasure of representing Australia, and despite these matches not being capped games, it didn't stop me from feeling the whole country was behind me. After seeing what

I went through in Darwin 2017 to qualify for the event, everyone was as excited as I was to see the day finally arrive.

I won my first five matches of the tournament, including a straight sets win over Martyn Rice from Scotland, and a tie-break win over Wayne Ritmuller from South Africa. In round six, little known Zimbabwean Aaron Chilundo drove me off the green in the first set, taking it nine shots to six. I won the second set comfortably after Aaron began to miss and decided to take the mat on the first end of the tie breaker and continue to play long. Out of nowhere, Aaron dobbed three bowls on the jack with no target and my attempts to hit the head missed. Chasing three shots in two ends to force a sudden death fourth end, I could only manage two singles and I'd cop my first singles blemish in Australian colours. The headlines on media sources that night had nothing to do with the fact I was still leading the section, but more that Zimbabwe had defeated Australia – and deservedly so. It was probably the loss I needed to get my concentration back on track.

My final seven matches of the tournament were all straight sets wins. I qualified on top of the table and earnt a spot directly into the World semi-finals. The benefit of finishing in top of the section was that even if you lost in the semi-final, you would be guaranteed a bronze medal. Being my first time in world level competition, I was thrilled to know that I would medal. The only question was what colour.

After Tony Cheung from Hong Kong beat Martyn Rice from Scotland in the quarter final, I knew my opponent for the semi-final. I was quietly confident I could win, knowing the rinks at St Johns Park were going to be up around 19 or 20 seconds and absolutely flying.

When we rolled up for our match, I noticed the green had been watered overnight and was down to around 15 seconds. It was by no means slow, but the wide draw and trickling finish had gone off the bowls. I was shattered. I knew Tony would be much harder to beat on that pace than the glass-like conditions of earlier days.

Somehow, I scored a couple of twos on the last couple of ends of the first set and snuck in seven shots to six. I wasn't playing anywhere near the standard I had been, and despite having one hand on a spot in the world final, my confidence was questionable. I played a lot of short first bowls, over-corrected long with my second bowl, and my drives were missing their target. There was nothing in my repertoire producing the goods.

At 6-7 down with one end to go in the second set, I only needed to score a single to win the match. I held the match with Tony having one bowl to play. To my devastation, he drove my shot bowl out clean as a whistle to win the second set and force a tiebreaker. The shot he played totally broke my heart. He played a great first end of the tie breaker and scored two, only to see me return the same score on him next end. Level with a single end to go in the match, Tony drew shot with his third bowl. My last bowl had to run Tony's bowl out to stay in the game and hope he failed with his last. There was no need for him to play his last, as my drive sailed wide of the target, catching nothing but clean air. I was out.

Initially upset and inconsolable after defeat, I later learnt to appreciate that I had won a world level medal. There was no way just fourteen months earlier that I could have ever imagined standing on a world dais watching my country's flag rise, with a bronze medal around my neck. I used to joke about bronze medals, saying they 'looked like gold medals that had been left outside in the rain and rusted'. But this was different. It was my first ever medal at world level and I would always be proud of that achievement. I was so close to that world final, but it wasn't to be.

Shannon McIlroy from New Zealand went on to beat Tony Cheung in the World final in straight sets, proving why he was known as one of the best singles players in the world. Tony had no answers from Shannon's consistent draw shot play and had to settle for the silver medal. The bowls die-hards all wanted to see a Schraner/McIlroy final, but with Tony too good the day before, their wishes went unanswered.

Rosny Park and Bendigo East both celebrated my bronze medal. From their point of view, it was the first time that any of their members had ever achieved a medal on a world stage and they were proud of my performance.

With another shot at the world title in Adelaide twelve months later, I was going to once again do everything I could to prepare for the championships. Opportunities at world level didn't come around often in the bowling world, so I became determined to do better than bronze the second time around.

Finally, I got my singles gold medal at the Victorian Open in 2018. Down 0-7 against Mark Foster from MCC in the final, I refused to be dealt a fourth silver. From that point on, I owned the match, running away with it 21-12. It was more of a relief than a celebration, but it did show I could win big singles finals when in trouble. It set the tone for my next attempt at the World's.

I wanted it so, so badly.

CHAPTER 44

Broken

Late November of 2018, I was invited to a Bowls Australia camp on the Gold Coast as part of the emerging jackaroos squad.

The camp was torture for me. We had to be up at 5:30am every morning and on the beach by 6:00am ready for the morning fitness program. Whether we stretched, threw tennis balls, or walked and ran kilometres on the sand, every player in the open and emerging squads had to be there. The sessions would often last for about 90 minutes, before heading back to our motel rooms for breakfast.

By 8:45am we were expected to meet at Broadbeach Bowling Club for a day of drills, match play, seminars, and one-on-one player interviews. After a morning playing in humid conditions, I was generally exhausted. The afternoon sessions were challenging and generally followed by seminars and dinner. Needing rest, I was often scheduled for my one-on-one meetings with the coach late in the day. I think the latest I had to stay back one night was well after 10:00pm. I couldn't even get six hours of sleep a night, meaning that by the end of the five days, I was on my last legs.

I wasn't sure if the camps were designed to test players and push them to their limits, or whether they were trying to prepare us for the exhaustion of competing in big events. Either way, I was the oldest player in the squads and certainly didn't appreciate the physical and mental burden. I'm not sure anyone did.

On the final day of the camp, we were treated with a trip to a skate park for an activity day. Some of the activities were a lot of fun, but some were also dangerous. I didn't want to participate in all the rotations but felt pressured to. If I didn't take part, I would look like an outlier and not part of the team. Anyone who didn't fit in with the team would be gone the next year without doubt. So, I had a go at everything.

When I first jumped on the trampoline, I knew it was a bad idea. With other people on the trampolines at the same time, every now and then I'd take a bounce many metres in the air and lose my co-ordination. Once it got too crowded, I decided to exit the apparatus as safely as possible. On an attempt to jump off safely into the foam pit, I flew uncontrollably the wrong direction and landed on the ground on my right foot.

I instantly felt pain, but I didn't want to show it. I knew I was hurt but did everything possible over the next few minutes to hide my distress.

Walking to the lunchroom, I couldn't place any weight on my right side without intense pain. I had developed a limp to protect my injured side, making sure I wouldn't do anymore damage than I'd already done. Other players, selectors and coaches all noticed I was injured, but I was never offered any treatment, nor a trip to the doctors or hospital.

When arriving at the airport for our flight home, I was put in a wheelchair in the Virgin lounge and given ice packs by airline staff to try and reduce the obvious swelling around my ankle. My skin had already started bruising and my ankle and foot had swollen so badly that I couldn't even put my shoe on. Even when boarding, I was placed in the makeshift elevator and wheeled onto the plane.

On arriving in Melbourne, I was picked up by Brad Marron and driven to Bendigo. After the flight, my ankle had exploded and there was no doubt I had broken something. I went straight to the hospital for an x-ray, but nothing appeared on the scan. I had the Australian singles and Australian triples finals in Merimbula the following week, and I was sure I wouldn't be able to play.

The hospital staff gave me anti-inflammatories and strapped my ankle, turning me away. I spent the night at Brad's in pain, unable to sleep from the discomfort.

I played pennant for Bendigo East that weekend off a fixed stance. I couldn't step forward and transfer my weight from one foot to another. My left side had to bear all the weight for me to deliver a bowl. I decided that even off a fixed stance, I would make the trip to Merimbula and attempt to play the Australian championships.

Once in Merimbula, I rolled up on their artificial greens using my fixed stance. Skipping the triples was going to be hard with Bag and Nutbush because I couldn't play any weighted shots. I was only able to draw from my fixed stance.

We lost our round one match to the ACT, and I played crap. I was also in agony. The next match against QLD, we decided that I would play lead, Bag second, and Nutbush take over the skipping role. It worked to some degree, but we lost in a close tussle. Against the NT in the final round, we knew our chances of playing for a medal were gone. I bit the bullet and took the skipping job back, winning the match with my final two bowls. At least we could walk away from the event winning one game.

I had two days to prepare for the Australian singles and hope that my ankle would give me some relief. I got myself some pain killers from the pharmacy, which I would rather not take, and began taking those the day before the event. They worked. I felt no pain in my right ankle but lost the feeling and touch in my hands. I was able to step to bowl but had to rely on my arm speed and wrist to get the correct weight, instead of the touch of my fingers.

I took so many pain killers the day of the singles championship that I was probably high as a kite. They were ASADA and WADA approved, so I had no issues being disqualified for illegal substances.

In the sectional play, I beat Jay Bye-Norris from VIC, Robert Craven from the ACT, and despite being 6-19 down in my last game, managed to come back and win against Mark Malgorski from the NT. Undefeated, I made the gold medal match against good friend and singles mastermind, Ray Pearse from NSW.

In an absorbing match going for over three hours, Ray would reach the magic number of 25 first and claim the gold medal. I was only a handful of shots off doing the Australian singles and Australian Champion of Champions singles double but fell agonisingly short. I'd proudly accept the silver medal, knowing I did everything physically possible in the match. Well over ten hours of bowls on a busted ankle in one day wasn't easy – especially high on pain killers.

I returned to Bendigo to play pennant before finally making the trip home to Hobart after more than two weeks away. The pain killers became addictive, and I knew it wasn't the long-term solution to my problem. Once home in West Moonah, I stopped taking them. Within hours of throwing them away, I developed intense pain in my ankle once more. Just looking at how swollen and purple it was should have been enough of a sign for doctors to treat it more seriously. It was time for answers.

I drove into the Hobart CBD and went through the emergency department. After triage, I was x-rayed, but again no fracture was visible. This time the doctor showed concern over the condition of my ankle and ordered an MRI scan immediately.

Within a couple of hours, I got the news that I had fractured my right talus (heel bone) in two places. This was a common bone to break when falling from heights, as it took the impact of all your body weight. A nurse wheeled in a trolley and started preparing to put a cast on my ankle. I wasn't interested in a cast and politely asked her to stop what she was doing. Apparently, I wasn't allowed to leave the hospital until my fracture had been treated, but I wasn't going in a cast. There were no 'moon boots' available until the doctor could see me the next day, so I checked myself out on a pair of crutches with a plan to return then.

I played a State series against the ACT in a moon boot not long after. Not only did we win the series 5-0, but my rink also won all five matches. In fact, for the three months I wore the boot, I didn't lose a single game of bowls. It probably made me concentrate harder than I ever had before, knowing everything had to be perfect in my delivery to keep my balance.

The week before the grand final in Bendigo, I finally got to take the boot off. Our side went on to beat Eaglehawk in a classic match, holding on by just 9 shots. Ironically, my rink would lose by the same margin to Darren Burgess. The other three rinks all had good wins and it was enough to cover our defeat. It topped off a season of many hours of hard work, travel, and coaching.

Bendigo East went on to make the State pennant final, comfortably beaten by Shepparton Golf in an all-country affair. It had been many years since a metropolitan Melbourne team had not made the State final. In a reverse from the grand final, my rink won, and all others lost. It started me thinking that I needed to lose my rink to win a team final.

But there was no logic in that.

CHAPTER 45

Bendigo

Bendigo East offered me a two-year extension on my coaching contract after the premiership success. Considering I paid for my own flights for a whole pennant season, I seriously started contemplating moving back to Victoria and living in Bendigo permanently.

I didn't make any decisions straight away, but the more I thought about it, the more I wanted to do it. I had been living in Tasmania for over five years and made many great friends. I had played 84 games for my new State and through success at a high level, earnt a place in the Australian emerging squad.

Rick and Deb had moved down to Dover to live, which was about an hour and a half from Moonah. Nutbush was planning a move to Perth to be closer to his parents, who were becoming frail in their old age. It seemed like everyone was moving away, so I decided to move as well.

When the news hit social media that I was returning to Victoria, I got a lot of emotional messages from people around Tasmania. They were all wishing me the best on my new adventure, but I could tell they didn't want me to go. The State selectors were still kind enough to select me for the Alley Shield at Ettalong, allowing me to have a 'swan song' in Tasmanian colours.

My final series was probably the most disappointing for our side. We won our first three matches against the ACT, SA, and WA, but lost the last four matches, including beltings from the NT, VIC, and QLD. We hadn't lost by margins like that for years and it affected the confidence of the whole team.

In the last match of the event, we played NSW. The team lifted for the final game, even though we were out of medal contention. In a spirited performance, we fell just a handful of shots short of causing an upset. I was proud of the team for their efforts and very grateful to have been on their side for all 91 games.

Many people thanked me for what I had brought to Tasmanian bowls. I saw the potential of the players we had in the State and knew we could be successful as a group. I taught the players to feel the pain of defeat, the thrill of winning, and that they should never accept an honourable loss. If they wanted to be a threat to the bigger States, they needed to learn how to win. I explained that Tasmania was not there to simply 'make up the numbers', they were there to take home the silverware. Once the side was instilled with the belief and confidence that they could do it, they became a threat to every team they played.

I remember thanking the players in a group huddle after my final match. I thanked them for making me fall back in love with the sport of lawn bowls, after losing interest some years earlier in Melbourne. I thanked them for making me feel the emotions of the game again. I thanked them for re-igniting my hunger to win. I even apologised for not drawing that final shot in Adelaide two years earlier, costing us the Alley shield. I told them that it wasn't what I'd done for Tasmanian bowls that was important, it was what Tasmanian bowls had done for me.

Two weeks after arriving back to Hobart from Ettalong, I made the move. I took nothing with me other than what could fit in my car, disposing of all my furniture and appliances. Brad Marron and his family were already in my Spring Gully unit putting together flat packs of my new furniture. Their help ensured that by the time I got there, I wouldn't need to do any work at all to be house ready.

My final night in Moonah was on the floor of my living room with pillows and a doona. Earlier that evening I had a small 'going away' party at the Valern to celebrate my time in Tasmania. I was so happy to see heaps of people make the effort to be there and it made me quite emotional. We told funny stories late into the night, sinking schooners of beer and reminiscing about the great times we had together. It was probably the best night I ever had.

I left late morning to make my way to the Spirit of Tasmania in Devonport. I wanted to be up there well before the 6:00pm departure time, so I could spend some time on the banks of the Mersey River, taking in one of the many beauties of the State. Devonport was one of my favourite spots in Tasmania and the view of the boat across the river confirmed why.

When five o'clock approached, I drove my car up to the waiting area and sat patiently. When it was my turn, I moved up the ramp and into the parking area. I made sure I got something to eat and drink before the boat exited the river into the Bass Strait. I didn't want to miss the view of Tasmania's north coast on the way out.

I stood at the rear of the boat on the upper deck. It was the same place I stood in 2014 when I left Station Pier in Port Melbourne. Once my food was finished, I lit a smoke and soaked up the view. As like last time, when my smoke reached the filter, I'd throw it away and light another one. I stared back at the shore as the sun disappeared over the distant horizon. The few lights visible on the land soon faded away in the darkness. The moment I lost sight of the coast was the moment I said my goodbye. The unforgettable cool breeze swept over the deck, and I made my way to the cabin door. Before entering, I shut my eyes and took a long, deep breath. I opened the door and took a step in before turning around one last time hoping to get the tiniest glimpse of Australia's most beautiful State, but it had been swallowed up by the darkness.

It was gone.

The announcement at 6:00am the next morning woke me up in the cabin. I grabbed my things and headed upstairs for a morning coffee. I got a great view of Melbourne as the sun rose. We were well into Port Phillip Bay and less than half an hour from docking. I spent that time on the front deck outside enjoying the scenery as we approached Station Pier.

It was just over two hours drive to Bendigo and I had to do it through Melbourne peak hour traffic. I certainly hadn't missed the gridlock of cars, especially after hardly experiencing any traffic at all in Hobart. It ended up taking me three hours to get to Bendigo, where I was greeted by Brad and his family at my unit. His mother-in-law had bought me a 'welcome' front door mat, which made me feel comfortable about my new place.

The unit was very new, well-maintained, and spacious. I had two bedrooms, a large kitchen and two bathrooms. My outdoor courtyard was private and perfect for one. My rent was relatively inexpensive for the condition of the property, so I was happy with my new place.

I started pinging someone online who caught my attention, but he would never respond. I didn't give up easily and continued messaging him until finally he sent a reply. His name was Chris, a blonde-haired, blue-eyed, short, and very attractive fella. We started messaging each other regularly until he finally agreed to meet. I lived across the road from the One Tree Hill hotel, a pub with pool tables and an outdoor entertainment area. We met there for a dinner date, where we instantly connected. He was 12 years younger than me but preferred older men. I wasn't complaining because I was generally attracted to younger men anyway.

He lived in Golden Square, about five kilometres from where I lived, but he didn't have a car. Well actually, he didn't even have a licence. He relied on taxis to get him to and from work, never interested in the slightest about getting his licence and owning a car. He was a café worker, starting early in the mornings and finishing mid-afternoon. He seemed very mature and organised for his age.

Chris and I began seeing each other regularly for dinner, where I would often cook something nice up for him. He fell in love with my cooking and as we began to get closer, he would come over more than once a week. I had been in minor relationships over my lifetime, but nothing that ever lasted very long. I wasn't interested in a sexual relationship, still very shy and protective of my body since my experiences in Bundoora many years before. I liked the company of men, but not the intimacy. I was living an asexual lifestyle and happy not to be physically involved with anyone.

I didn't have to explain myself to Chris. He liked me for who I was and was more than willing to give the relationship a go. Five years on we are still together and happier than ever before, living with our three cats Irene, Maximilian, and Oscar. The cats are our children and Chris does an amazing job looking after them.

By July 2019, I was eagerly awaiting the announcement of the Australian teams and hopeful I could take a step up from the emerging squad into the main squad. The text message was sent out to all current squad members as well as new ones. I didn't make the open squad unfortunately, but worse still, I was dropped from the emerging squad. I was told that the emerging squad was redesigned to introduce younger players with the potential of playing for Australia in future years. At 37 years of age, I was not in their plans going forward, so was omitted from the squads.

I became angry and frustrated, having won the Australian Champion of Champions singles back-to-back, a World bronze medal and the Tasmanian State fours while a part of the squad. I thought there were enough runs on the board to be promoted to the open squad, so I was in disbelief when I was left out altogether. I sent emails to the Australian coach seeking further explanation of my omission but was only dealt political and democratic responses. Being as old as I was and noting that only one player in the squads was 40, I did the respectful thing and retired indefinitely. I had to put the dream of playing for Australia to bed and focus on my upcoming stint at the World Champion of Champions singles in Adelaide. Even though they weren't capped matches, it seemed the only way I was ever going to wear the uniform again. Rather than go on whining about being dropped, I developed even more determination to win the world title and prove to myself that I was up to the standard required to play International level bowls.

I never played bowls to prove other people wrong. I always played to prove myself right. I doubted myself because of the lack of opportunity I had been given by National selectors. I was always questioning why they were leaving me out and not giving me a go. Maybe I wasn't good enough to play for Australia and my selection in the emerging team was just a token of congratulations for the previous couple of years of success. Or maybe I was just picked in the team to give the main squad players some singles competition. It is easy to doubt yourself when you don't have the support of the ones who decide whether you play for Australia or not.

Selection is only someone else's opinion.

CHAPTER 46

Triumph

I chose not to work in Bendigo. With my coaching income and pension, I could live comfortably without needing the extra income. The main reason behind not working was so I could spend every day on the bowling green training for the Worlds in Adelaide.

I cannot tell you how many hours I put into my game. I just wanted to make sure I would be as prepared as possible for the event, to see whether I was good enough or not to take the next step. If I had done the work and found out I wasn't good enough, then I could get on with life without any regrets. It was most likely my last shot at a world title, so I was doing everything in my power to be ready for the opportunity.

The season started well once again in Bendigo, with the side winning almost every match. We were certainly on track to make it back-to-back premierships.

Two weeks before the Worlds, I was upset in the second round of the club singles by Martin Lord 25-13. He was the champion from the year before, but with all the training I had been doing, I was expected to win the club singles. It put a halt to my run at the State and National Champion of Champions singles, missing out on both events for the first time in three years.

That loss highlighted weaknesses in my game that I had to iron out immediately. My training had been so focused on draw bowling, that I'd neglected to train enough weighted shots. I incorporated more of those shots into my final two weeks of training and made sure my whole game was in perfect order for Adelaide.

There was no doubt I had the favoured of the two sections for the championship. Section one included New Zealand, Scotland, England, Namibia, Malaysia, and my nemesis from twelve months earlier, Tony Cheung from Hong Kong. My section included Ireland, South Africa, Wales, and the United States, but I had eight matches against minnow nations, namely Botswana, Fiji, Guernsey, Israel, Japan, Norfolk Island, Singapore, and Turkey. My section would surely be decided by the results against the more established Nations.

After a sloppy straight sets win over Kwok Fai Law from Singapore in round one, I found myself in all sorts of trouble against Wayne Rittmuller from South Africa. At 4-4 going into the last end of the second set, I had to win it to force a tiebreaker after dropping the first. Down on the head with one bowl to play, I drew shot and saved the match. The tiebreaker was strange in the fact that I only played two ends to lead 5-0, and was unable to be caught with an end to spare.

I snapped into form by round three beating Hirokazi Mori from Japan comfortably in straight sets, and then fought off a determined Ozkan Akar from Turkey in two close sets. Having already got past one of the biggest threats, Rittmuller, round five would be equally important against Charlie Herbert from the United States. It was a match to remember, winning the first set by six shots, only to drop the second set by the same margin. At 1-1 in the tiebreaker with just one end remaining, Charlie drove the jack in the ditch with his first bowl and sat just two feet away. I drew the shot the plinth with my second bowl, only to see Charlie drive it out. I repeated the dose with my third bowl and didn't want to have to play my last. Charlie's attempt grazed my shot bowl, but it stayed on the playing surface and the match was mine with a bowl to spare.

My run to the finals was not as comfortable as it was the previous year, but my play during the tiebreakers was producing all the winners. I was surprising myself with some of the shots I was executing, especially without nerves or the fear of losing. I was relaxed because I was prepared, and this was evident in round six against Kevin James from Wales. In a game where I felt I was out-played, I managed to win the first set 10-6 before dropping the second set 8-11. In the tiebreaker, I produced one magic draw shot each end that helped secure a 3-0 scoreline and leave me undefeated in the championships. With Wales, South Africa, and the United States all now beaten, I was sure to make the top three and qualify for the finals. Having dropped three sets meant I had to keep on winning to stay on top of the ladder. By finishing first in the section, I'd guarantee another world medal and a spot in the semi-finals.

In the seventh round I played Regent Reid from Botswana. It was an uncomfortable first set, with not much going my way. I managed to hold on, before winning comfortably in the second. Round eight was against Rajnesh Prasad from Fiji and it was probably the best I had played all week. I won the first set 15-1, but to Rajnesh's credit, he played brilliantly in the second set. It was a very high standard match. At 8-8 and just a single bowl to play, Rajnesh had a bowl an inch off the jack directly in front. He also had the bowl at the back of the rink and on the re-spot. I had no shot but to attempt to draw it cold – and I did, a resting side toucher for the set and match!

With eight wins in the bag, I had just four matches to go before finals. I beat Markus Boaz from Israel in round nine in straight sets, then Stephen Coleman from Ireland with a similar scoreline, and appeared on track to do the same to Todd Priaux from Guernsey when I ran away with the first set 19-2. In a frustrating second set, I was pipped 8-9, and despite scoring 27 shots to 11 in the match, I was forced into a tiebreaker. In a weird turn of events, Todd missed the draw weight completely with all four bowls on the first end, and I scored a maximum count. I put my first two bowls close on the second end and watched as Todd fired with his last two bowls, only to drive all his own bowls off the green. The match was done with an 8-0 tiebreaker score after just two ends.

I sat out round twelve with a bye and finished my undefeated section run in round thirteen against good friend Haydn 'Teddy' Evans from Norfolk Island. By remaining undefeated, I finished first in the section and guaranteed myself another world medal – it was just a matter of what colour it would be.

The following day, Louis Ridout from England beat Charlie Herbert from the United States to take a spot in the semi-final against me. In the other match, Tony Cheung from Hong Kong beat South African Wayne Rittmuller, booking a spot in the other semi-final against Mark O'Hagan from Scotland.

My match against Louis gave me my first dose of nerves for the week. I didn't want to go out in the semi-final two years running, so put those thoughts aside and focused purely on each bowl I played. There was no doubt that Louis wasn't on form for the match, and I ran away with it 9-3, 11-3. I sat there afterwards watching the end of Mark and Tony's game, praying to every source possible that Mark would win. I didn't want to face Tony in the final. I knew if he was my opponent that nerves would kick in and I'd have to deal with the constant reminder of the result one year earlier.

Tony played an unbelievable shot on the last end of the second set to win the match, qualifying for the World final for the second year running.

That night, I thought carefully about my game plan and how to deal with Tony. It was a known fact that he is one of the slowest players in the world and this can annoy and affect his opponents. I decided to treat the final as a celebration and to enjoy every minute of it. If he was going to be slow, I was going to be even slower. A normal game took about an hour and a half, but I was preparing for at least an extra hour on top of that. It was important to realise that the game would take ages to finish, knowing I had to maintain concentration longer than I normally would have to.

I woke on the morning of finals day to a knock at my hotel room door. Curious as to why someone was waking me up at 8:30am when the final wasn't until 2:00pm, I opened the door. There, stood Brad Marron, his wife and mother-in-law, who had driven through the night from Bendigo to Adelaide to watch the final live. If that wasn't enough to wake me up, Mum jumped out from behind the wall and surprised me too. She too had spent most of the night in the car, making the seven-and-a-half-hour journey with them.

I went to the club early to watch the women's final between Debbie White from New Zealand and Kylie Whitehead from Australia. It was a thrilling match, going down to the final end of the tie-breaker. After Debbie's last bowl narrowly missed, Kylie became a world champion. It was awesome to watch her excitement when she realised the gold medal was hers. It certainly gave me a few butterflies.

The green was rolled several times before our final and started at around 17 seconds. The wind was inconsistent and swirling around, so the match wasn't expected to be the highest quality. I was happy that the green was quick, knowing it would affect some of Tony's shot play.

The first set was a titanic battle. In the nine ends, I dropped six singles, but in the three ends I won, I scored three, two, and two. The first set was mine 7-6.

The second set was all about Tony showing his class. He flew out of the blocks and scored seven before I got on the board. Despite all my efforts to chase him down, I fell narrowly short 6-9.

It was a three-end tiebreaker to decide the World singles champion. I held shots on the first end only to see Tony convert the head in his favour. My last bowl failed, and Tony took the lead 1-0. The second end I trailed the jack away from Tony's bowls into open territory, only to see him play a great draw shot near the boundary line. I had second shot and was tempted to try and drive his bowl out with my last. After an eternity of deliberation, I went back to the mat convinced I had to try and draw it. Tony's bowl was a terrific shot, but mine was even better. I stopped just in time, about a foot away from the jack for shot bowl.

It was now a one-end shootout to decide the World singles champion.

I threw a short-end, not confident of beating Tony over full-length. My first bowl was slightly wide, and he took advantage, drawing a shot right next to the jack. I drove the jack in the ditch with my second bowl, but my toucher was not close enough to be the winner. After Tony's second bowl fell in the ditch, I asked the marker if I could walk to the head. When I need to bowl outside of the rink, I like to walk my line and inspect whether the unused grass will require me to add weight to the delivery or not. I saw nothing that caught my attention, so I delivered the bowl as normal.

I chased the bowl down the green, which for anyone who knows me well, is a very rare thing for me to do. The bowl drew right up to the edge of the ditch and stopped less than a foot from the edge, right in line with the jack. It was a cracker!

Tony drew second shot with his third bowl, meaning I needed to add another shot. If I failed, he could drive my shot bowl out with his last and steal the match. I added another shot and gave him no target to work with.

I stood at the mat end gazing into Rymill Park at the people going about their daily business. I held the world title in my hands and had no ammunition left. It was there for Tony to break my heart. Emotion got the better of me and while looking into the park, I began to feel tears running down my cheeks. In my opinion, I had just played the last bowl I would ever play in Australian colours. I truly believed that it was my last shot at a world title and that I would never make it back to the world finals again.

Tony lined up and tried to drive both my bowls out. I turned around to watch his shot, eyes blurry and my cheeks red from tears. He was clearly wide of his target, and I began to feel excited, only to see his errant drive ricochet off his previous bowl and end up only a millimetre away from fluking the world title.

I screamed in delight.

I fell to my knees, head in hands.

I was completely overwhelmed.

Mum came and gave me a hug. I looked at her and all I could say was, "I can die happy now. I've conquered the world". I got a lot of hugs and handshakes from people in the crowd, including Brad and his family.

I cannot describe the unbelievable feeling of winning a world title and standing on the top of a dais singing your National anthem. For those few moments, everyone is looking up at you. It literally feels like you are standing atop Mount Everest – on top of the world! It was without doubt, the greatest moment in my life.

I now had the unusual record of having more world level medals than capped matches for Australia. I was a world singles champion just four months after being dropped from the Australian emerging squad. Fourteen matches of singles in six days and fourteen wins on the world stage. It made me think a lot about playing for Australia again and having the confidence that I could win the big matches. It was more of a dream than a reality, but I didn't have to prove anything to anyone anymore. If they didn't want to pick me, there was nothing greater I could do to try and change their minds.

They never did.

CHAPTER 47

Lost

You'd think the best thing that ever happened to me would be winning a World title. Unfortunately, after I was home for a few days, I became totally lost in life.

I'd spent so much time training for the Worlds that suddenly, now it was won, I had way too much time on my hands. I often sat at home pondering what I wanted to do next with my life. The thinking was dangerous, and it started to have an affect on my mental health. Chris was first to notice my depression and offered to help me in any way he could. There was nothing he could do though. I had to figure it out myself.

I became a registered BAS Agent and began my own bookkeeping business from home. My initial target market was Uber drivers, who had to register for GST whether they reached the thresholds or not. Despite language barriers with some of my clients, I was able to give them peace of mind for less than $100 a quarter. It wasn't a big money-making enterprise, but it helped me discover a new goal.

In Merimbula that December, I played in the Australian fours with my Tasmanian team that won the state title in January. In a shock to the finalists, we won all three sectional matches against VIC, WA, and QLD. Expecting to play NSW in the final, we sat back in amazement as SA knocked them off in the final sectional match, allowing the NT through on margin.

It was the first time in history that Tasmania had played the Northern Territory in a National men's fours final. We weren't going to let the opportunity slip, winning a low scoring 15 end final 14-7. I finally had a National title in fours after so many years. Known predominantly as a four-bowl player, it was nice to collect a gold medal using just two; and skipping too.

By early 2020, the Covid-19 pandemic had become our lives. It was just a matter of time before the Victorian Premier locked down the State.

Bendigo East made the grand final played in March but were demolished by South Bendigo on a ridiculously quick surface at Golden Square. Our dream of back-to-back premierships was halted by an up-and-coming side, who would go on to win the next two premierships in Bendigo pennant.

Just a fortnight after our devastating loss, Dan Andrews locked down Victoria. We were faced with astronomical restrictions and stuck like house-hermits for 43 days. All my clients were unable to drive their Ubers, so I lost every single one of them. My business was basically broke. Couple that with State championships being postponed indefinitely, I found myself in a very low place.

Chris and I were able to see each other during the lockdown, which made sure I wouldn't go completely insane. Without any work to do, the inability to play bowls, and nothing to keep me entertained, my days were long and slow. All I could do was watch shows on Netflix to fill in the time, making sure I tuned in on television every day for the address from our Premier.

Every day I would hold my breath hoping he would let us out of lockdown. We were allowed out by the middle of May, but only under certain conditions. No longer did I just have to check for phone, wallet, keys, and smokes when I left the house, I had to make sure I had a mask too.

Regional Victoria was not in lockdown as long as Melbourne, nor did we have all the restrictions placed on metropolitan residents, but it didn't detract from being a nightmare.

When we re-opened, I played a pennant match for Raymond Terrace in Newcastle, as a fly-in marquee player. The match fee was good, so I had no problem accepting their offer.

On the 9th of July, we were again placed in lockdown. After just one match with Raymond Terrace, there would be no more for the season. Our second lockdown in Victoria lasted a whopping 111 days. There was only so much television and Netflix you can watch before it becomes more of a chore than a pleasure. Life was as boring as it got. Living became merely existing.

To fill time, I took on the bar management volunteer position at Bendigo East and spent many days reconfiguring the till system and stock. The bowling club wasn't open, so I could venture down to the club alone and work there.

Bendigo was let out of lockdown earlier than Melbourne, as well as other regional areas. We were able to play bowls but had to do so in a mask. I don't know how many masks I went through by accidentally burning holes in them with cigarettes. It was a ridiculous situation being outside and having to wear a mask. In any event, most of us were just happy to be allowed out of the house.

We got our bowls season under way, but under tight social distancing measures. The state championships were re-scheduled for January 2021 and moved from Bendigo to Warrnambool.

Over Christmas, Brad Marron and I had a fallout over team selection and he and his wife were given clearances from Bendigo East and asked to leave. With the State pairs just a month away, it wasn't a guarantee that we would step on the green together. Neither of us wanted to give up our spot for a substitute, so we were forced to deal with each other. To be a chance at winning, we made the deal to be best mates on the green, while off the green we hardly spoke.

Our plan worked, as we went to Warrnambool and won the State pairs gold medal. I followed it up just a couple of days later by winning the State singles gold medal as well. If Covid stayed away, I'd have the opportunity of playing in two events at the Australian championships scheduled for May at Dandenong Club. The new dates would follow Victoria's 2021 State champions week, which was back at Bendigo East once more.

I signed on for Raymond Terrace again in 2021, hoping my fly-in agreement would last more than a single game this time around. The money was good, and the team was as good as any I had ever played in. For a regional club, they were always up there with the big Sydney clubs when State pennants were on the line.

The club went one step further and invited me and Chris up for a day in late February. The club knew I was not happy in Bendigo and had spoken to Chris about moving back to Hobart. He was interested in the idea, believing it was time to get out of Bendigo. I was 95% sure at the time that Tasmania would be home again, willing to fly up to Raymond Terrace for pennant. Their quick actions proved to be a genius move.

We knew in advance that Chris was going for a job interview, with the club trying to secure him so I'd move to Newcastle full-time.

Their goal was to give him an offer he couldn't refuse so that he'd want to move interstate. Wherever Chris went, I was going. If he stayed in Bendigo, I would too. If he wanted to go to Tasmania, I was following him. If he decided he liked the offer from Raymond Terrace, then I'd go there with him.

After Chris's interview and tour of Newcastle, I was still convinced we were moving to Tasmania. Within a few days, Chris told me straight out that he was accepting the front of house manager position in the restaurant and wanted to make the move to Raymond Terrace, whether I wanted to or not. It was Chris who made the call to move to Newcastle, not me. He was the driver behind our decision to come to New South Wales together.

Our move was planned for 1st June, just a few days after the Australian championships finished in Dandenong. We started packing up our houses in March, wanting to be prepared for the move. Chris was working two jobs in an effort to save some money, while I was saving every dollar I could. The club paid for our moving expenses, but we needed to come up with money for rent and a bond on a rental property we liked in Tanilba Bay, about half an hour from Raymond Terrace.

When champions week came, I had a great run in the State Champion of Champions singles once more. After winning my first round against Ben Loughlin from Altona, I then knocked off the previous year's winner Rhys Jeffs in the quarter final. My semi final was against Brendan Umbers, and after a slow start, I ran away with that match too.

Lining up against Ali Forsyth on a bowling green is scary at the best of times but meeting him in the State final was very intimidating. Ali is one of the best players to ever play the sport. He has multiple World championships and hundreds of representative caps for New Zealand. I was able to fight off the nerves and burst out of the blocks. I maintained my 10-shot lead for most of the game and finished off with a string of ones. It was my seventh State Champion of Champions singles gold medal, but more importantly, had me on the same wins as Australian legend Glynn Bosisto. I made it my aim to chase him down when I won my second title in 2009, but I never thought I'd reach him in just another twelve years.

Dandenong arrived quickly and National titles were on the line. Brad and I qualified for the pairs final despite losing our last match, with my final drive removing three of our opposition's shot bowls to get through the section on margin. We played Chris LeLievre and Matt Lucas from QLD in the National final that evening, being one of the best games I had ever played. We led 19-1 at one stage and were never headed, finishing the match two ends ahead of schedule. Not only did Brad and I come down from Bendigo in separate cars, we also didn't stay together in a hotel. We never really spoke much at all after the game, sticking to the same plan as the State finals in Warrnambool.

Feeling good and looking forward to the singles, Covid threw a massive spanner in the works. Just one day before the event started, there was whisper about the State being locked down. All the competitors jumped on planes to get home, and the event was called off. The Premier was threatening to put the State under lockdown once more. Chris and I had just five days until our move, and panic immediately set in. If Dan Andrews locked down Victoria, we wouldn't be able to make our scheduled move to Tanilba Bay. I had to think; and think fast!

I rang Chris immediately at work and told him to get home and pack his essentials. The border was shutting at 4:30pm and we had only five hours to get into New South Wales. Chris organised his Mum to finish our bond cleaning and to meet the removalists at both our houses. We had to get out of Victoria, or we would be stuck there, with lockdown leaving us liable to pay rent on both our Bendigo houses and our Tanilba Bay house. The rent in Tanilba Bay was $600 a week, so it wasn't a debt we wanted to incur.

The bowling club offered Chris and I free accommodation at the club's bed and breakfast for as many nights as we needed. We weren't allowed in the new house for five days, so had to stay somewhere when arriving in Newcastle. I threw my clothes in the car as well as my cat Max and drove to Golden Square to pick Chris up. He tossed his stuff in the car and grabbed his cat, Irene. We fed them their sleeping tablets in preparation for the long car drive and took off down the road.

It all happened so fast. We didn't have time to scratch ourselves.

We crossed the border into New South Wales before deadline, but by less than an hour. The eleven-hour drive to Raymond Terrace involved many stops along the highway to refill on coffee. I was very tired by midnight but with four hours to go, I had to stay awake and focused on the road.

By the time we reached Sydney, the cats had woken up from their sleep. They cried all the way to Raymond Terrace, annoying, but it kept me wide awake. We arrived at 3:45am and found the hidden key left for us using Chris's phone torch. After tossing the cats inside, giving them a feed and setting up a litter tray, we went to bed exhausted.

We made it.

CHAPTER 48

Terrace

The cats found a spot on the windowsill where they could lay down in the sunlight. Chris and I never left the accommodation for five days, choosing to self-isolate from others in case we had Covid. We weren't required by law to do it, but we wanted to do it anyway.

Our belongings were collected by the removalist and due for delivery the following day, so we made our way to Tanilba Bay where Chris could get his first look at the property. This house was a mansion. It was two stories with a massive upstairs balcony, two bathrooms and three bedrooms. We sat just metres away from the water, able to see it clearly from our balcony. It was the nicest house I had ever lived.

The removalist didn't show up on time the following day. We waited hours for them to arrive, only to hear the truck clip a power pole across the road just after midnight. The two removalists unloaded the truck over the next couple of hours, filling our house with furniture and appliances. They left Chris's fridge in Bendigo, which was annoying, with mine sold before making the trip.

After finally getting all our stuff inside, we could relax and enjoy our new house.

Chris caught the bus every morning to work but needed me to pick him up afterwards. The buses didn't run late enough from Raymond Terrace to Tanilba Bay, so I offered to pick him up each night. I was hoping he could get a car and licence by Christmas.

By August, our state premier Gladys Berejiklian hinted that Newcastle and the Hunter Valley, was about to be locked down for Covid. Sydney had been in lockdown since late June, and we were expecting the worst. We ended up in lockdown for almost three months, unable to escape the Covid pandemic in our new State.

Out of boredom, I started a small business in my garage making flavoured crumbs. It seemed like a good idea at the time, but through Covid, it was impossible to make a profit. I had a small peak early in 2022, but ultimately closed it down in June.

By April, Raymond Terrace had won the premiership and qualified for State pennant finals later that year. I'd miss the opportunity to play in it with them, coming across an unfortunate clash of events. I went to Broadbeach to play the delayed 2021 Champion of Champions singles National finals, winning all seven matches and claiming the gold medal for a record third time. The world finals were set for Wellington at the same time the State pennant finals were on. I wasn't going to miss the Worlds.

I debuted for New South Wales as a second, playing State bowls alongside my great mate Matt Baus. We fell just short at the Alley Shield, and it was an eleventh silver medal for me at the event. I later skipped against Victoria in July (due to players being involved in the Commonwealth Games in England), and that's where I stayed moving forward.

In April 2022, my cat Max went missing. He was an outdoor cat so went outside every day, coming in at night to sleep on the bed. After four weeks gone, I decided to surprise Chris with a brand-new kitten. Irene had started to fret and was lonely. She needed a friend to have around the house. I picked up a nine-week-old kitten from Newcastle and named him Oscar. Chris was so happy to see a second cat in the house, and so was Irene.

A week after Oscar arrived, Max appeared at the rear door crying at the top of his voice. He was grossly thin and unwell. I let him inside and tried to pick him up, but he ran straight to the food bowl and started gulping. He ate so fast that he vomited, only to repeat the dose a couple more times. I couldn't believe he was alive! I thought he was a goner for sure.

We later worked out that Max had been accidentally locked in a neighbour's garage when they went on holiday. He had access to a water source but had no food for almost five weeks. I took close care of him for the next few weeks, watching him slowly add weight. It was so good to have my kitty back.

Max and Oscar didn't get along at all. Max constantly hissed at him, clearly upset that another male cat was in the house. Eventually they became friends, play-fighting and sleeping on the bed together. We now had three cats to take care of.

Our time in Tanilba Bay was only for twelve months. The fishing was great, the view incredible, the area magnificent, and the neighbours were very friendly. With Chris working six to seven days per week, I made the call that we needed to be closer to the club. The fuel costs of picking him up daily began to add up, and the times he was finishing were getting later and later. I began having trouble driving at night with my eyesight, so didn't want to make the trips anymore.

A house became available across the road from the bowling club, giving Chris a one-minute walk to work. It also meant that between lunch and dinner shifts, he could come home, eat lunch and rest. There was no need for him to wait around for two or three hours until the dinner shift. The club owned the house, so we were able to organise a rental agreement with them straight away.

It rained constantly the week before we moved. The streets around the club were all under at least a metre of water after the Hunter Riverbank broke. Our house was safe on an elevated hill, but the surrounding land was completely flooded. If the rain didn't stop soon, we would not be able to move on our scheduled day.

When the rain stopped, it took three days for the water levels to drop. Many people in the area were stuck cleaning up damage to their properties and removing ruined carpet and furniture. Our house never had a drop of water inside it. The water level got very close to sliding under the front door, but never reached quite high enough. The driveway was mud, so moving was an interesting experience.

Brad Griffiths came up from Melbourne to help us with the move. Without his lifting of the heavy stuff up the stairs, we would have had no hope getting everything inside. After a very long day of shifting, we finished the job. We were now residents of Raymond Terrace, one kick of the football from the bowling club.

We were home.

CHAPTER 49

History

I left for Wellington after a month of intense training at Raymond Terrace. Knowing New Zealand conditions would be fast and windy, I made sure I worked extremely hard on weighted shots before I went. In those type of conditions, you needed to be able to hit regularly.

My tournament was probably the best I'd played in my three attempts but wouldn't get me the gold medal. I won all ten sectional matches, including eight in straight sets, but failed to get over the line in the semi-final. With the wind speeds over 70km/h outside, the blazers decided to move the event finals to the indoor green. Izzat Dzulkeple from Malaysia put on a masterclass on the indoor carpet, smashing me off the rink in straight sets. I was extremely upset about moving the event indoors after playing my heart out in the wind for four days prior. I felt I had a better chance of winning outside, rather than on the indoor green.

Dzulkeple lost the final to Sam Tolchard from England, which funnily enough was played outside. In gusty conditions, on a lightning quick green, Sam won the match with his very last bowl in the tiebreaker. I'd have to settle for bronze; a third world medal.

While I was in Wellington, Raymond Terrace won the one grade state pennant, beating Warilla in the final by a single shot. It was a mighty performance from the team, bearing in mind that we had no fly-in marquee players, and I was absent too.

Chris and I took some time off over Christmas and caught up with family in Victoria. It was the break from bowls I needed after the disappointment of the World championships bronze. I had plans for a bigger and better year and the break helped me work out what I wanted to achieve.

Without doubt, the best bowling year of my life was 2023. I hadn't been to an Australian Open in years, finding a balance between my bookkeeping work, family, and bowls. Chris and I decided that while the Australian Open was on, we could get away for two weeks somewhere away from work and bowls. I look forward to our holiday every year.

Raymond Terrace won the Newcastle pennant again and went on to make it back-to-back State pennants. Our two grade also won the State flag, putting our club in elite company. Aron Sheriff joined us as a fly-in marquee and certainly helped us get over the line in the State pennant final. It was nice to be part of the win this time around.

Matt Baus and I won every game for four days in the finals of the New South Wales Champion of Champions pairs and took the gold medal. It was Matt's first State pairs win, so made the moment even more special.

Following that, I went through another four days undefeated in the New South Wales Champion of Champions singles, claiming my eighth state title in the event. The final was a classic against Jake Lawton from East Maitland, where I came out on top 25-24 in a thriller. The win gave me a ticket to the National Champion of Champions singles later that year in Perth and an opportunity to win an unprecedented fourth National championship in the same event.

I scored an invite to the Golden Nugget Prestige singles at Tweed Heads for the first time in over a decade. After getting through my section in the top three, I had to reel off wins against Aaron Teys, Corey Wedlock, and in the final, Aron Sheriff, to take home the chocolates. With the conditions windy at times, I was drawing consistently and hitting well, keeping me in every match I played. I liked playing in the wind because it suited my draw/drive style of singles. There was also no re-spot of the jack for dead ends, so it was good old-fashioned singles play.

My trip to Perth ended up being the most perfect trip imaginable. I lost round one to Daniel Baker from the NT before winning every other game. It was enough to seal the gold medal for a fourth time and once again qualify for the World Champion of Champions late in 2024, in Auckland, New Zealand.

The Alley Shield that followed finally got me the gold medal I so desperately needed. Skipping for New South Wales, both the side and my rink when undefeated for all seven matches, giving me a double-gold in the event. Our state lost just one rink out of 21 in a dominant performance.

My bowls was good, my health the best it had ever been, and I was generally happy with life. Chris and I continue to live in the same house in Raymond Terrace where we are more than content. I may drink too much from time-to-time or stay out a bit late on a day off, but one thing is for certain, I am living my life. No longer do I let mental illness control me. I know it's there, but it doesn't run my life anymore.

Winning in Adelaide in 2019 taught me to believe in myself. I may have off days here and there on the green and in general life, but it will never stop me from losing my self-confidence. Even when times seem tough, I continue to remain positive and appreciative of life.

I have met a lot of new friends since my move to New South Wales. They have become a family to me. I don't care how good or bad they are at lawn bowls; they are bloody good people. Everyone needs a close group of friends like that who stick together. Our special table at the bowling club becomes a Mecca of fun every time we meet over a beer, wine, or my latest favourite, tawny port.

Maybe I have these new friends because I'm a likeable person.

Maybe they need me as much as I need them.

Maybe I was meant to be up here all along.

Even though sport is a massive part of my existence, there is a lot more to life than lawn bowls. Without it, I may not have survived my mental breakdowns. Without mental illness, I would never have become as tough as I am in sport. As bizarre as it sounds, I am grateful for experiencing both. They made me who I am today.

The ace of spades belonged in my life.

No-one has the heart and determination on a bowling green like I do. No-one compares. I never give up until my very last bowl has been played, and I plan to continue doing so until the day I die.

Everything happens for a reason.

CHAPTER 50

Life

Of all the moments in my life, nothing will ever compare to that magical day in Adelaide. That Sunday, I took life head-on, and prevailed.

I had been at a crossroads too many times.

For most of my life, I'd lived the hell of mental illness.

I knew what it was like attempting to live as a gay man, in a straight world.

My addictions to cigarettes and gambling had threatened to tear me apart.

My financial ebbs and flows saw me homeless, unemployed at times, often without a decent meal, and totally at rock bottom.

My general hate for who I was as a human being had exhausted me for the last time.

Yet, everything I had been through would all become worthwhile.

When Tony Cheung's last bowl of the tiebreaker narrowly missed, a stunning moment in history was created. Without having a second to think about the result, I screamed to the sky in an absolute moment of pleasure and relief. The spine-tingling shriek set all my demons free. I knew this meant a lot, but the real impact hadn't registered just yet.

I could hardly move from the thrill. My legs were shaking, my body was numb, and I was crying uncontrollably. I collapsed to the ground, unable to stay on my feet.

I had just won the World singles. It would be the icing on a 25-year sporting career. It couldn't get any better than that, surely.

My victory was much more than just a gold medal. For my whole life I had been trying to understand the purpose of my existence; the reason why I had fought so hard to stay on the planet. Bowls was my outlet from reality. It was the time I could be who I really wanted to be in life. I was a leader, a mentor, confident, special, unique, happy, satisfied, and free from mental illness. I was simply known as 'Leeroy', the man everyone wanted to beat.

Standing on top of the World helped me realise a lot of things.

I learnt that I could achieve anything in life moving forward.

I knew that planning, training, and working harder than anybody else, gave me the best chance of being successful.

I understood that preparing for matches in my own way would give me my best possible performance.

The law of attraction made me feel one with the world. I had visualised that moment for years.

I truly believed that good things came to those who deserved them.

This wasn't luck; this was fate.

I began to accept who I was as a human being.

That night in the hotel room, the realisation started to sink in. My exhausted mind and body could no longer cope. I wasn't sure if becoming a World champion had hit home, or whether I had finally caught up to life itself. The bubble finally burst. I cried tears of joy well past the midnight hour, until eventually I ran dry, and drifted off to sleep.

Life for me was not complete, but a devastatingly long chapter was closing. There had been many rough roads travelled over the years, but the tarmac was getting smoother by the day.

My whole motto in life was never to try and prove other people wrong; it was always about trying to prove myself right. I needed an answer to justify my existence.

My self-doubt left forever in Adelaide.

For the first time, I could honestly look at myself in the mirror and be proud of who I saw. Words cannot describe the realisation of being able to accept yourself for who you are. No longer did I see myself as inferior, a mental case, a smoker, a gambler, a poofter, or a psycho. I saw myself as the whole package and not a label. These things made me who I was.

The acceptance of who I was in life was my greatest ever achievement. I truly believed from the bottom of my heart, that I had exorcised my demons and freed myself from self-hate. No-one could ever take that away from me.

I finally believed I knew the meaning of life.

No matter what anyone else said or thought, it didn't matter.

To me, at last, I had *Nothing to Prove*.

ABOUT THE AUTHOR

Lee Schraner is a previous Australian International representative, and World Champion of Champions singles gold and dual bronze medallist in lawn bowls. He is the only player in Australian history to have more world level medals than capped matches for his country.

Throughout his career, Lee began keeping notes on a wide variety of topics. Many of these subjects provided the basis for the release of "In the Zone – Mental Toughness in Lawn Bowls" in 2014.

Lee is a an openly gay athlete. He was diagnosed with anxiety disorder, psychomotor retardation, and depression in 2003. His mental illness often left him incapacitated, confused, and even suicidal. Over the course of his illness, he learnt to take control of his thoughts by dismissing all disruptive and negative feelings, choosing only to act on anything constructive and positive. His road to recovery helped pave the way for an unquestionable mental toughness in his sport and life.

Through his life, he has gained a lot of admirers and fans in lawn bowls. Many of these people have confided in Lee on their personal battles with mental illness, trusting he could help them through their darkest days.

Lee played only one official test match for Australia in 2010 before being omitted from the squad prior to the 2010 Commonwealth Games in Delhi, India.

He has represented Australia at Under 25 level on 12 occasions and played 39 games for Australia at the World Champion of Champions in 2018, 2019, and 2022. In total, he has represented Australia 52 times. Lee lost just 7 of his 52 matches in Australian colours and just 3 of his 42 singles matches, highlighting an 86% overall International win record, and an unprecedented 93% International singles win record.

Lee continues to play State bowls after 20 years and 330 test matches, showing no signs of relenting his position soon. He remains the oldest current player in the New South Wales Men's team, at 42 years of age.

Today, Lee lives with his partner Chris, and their three cats, Max, Irene, and Oscar, in Raymond Terrace, a regional area about 30 minutes north-west of Newcastle. He enjoys fishing, writing, and working as a BAS Agent from home.

He still struggles from time-to-time with his mental deficiencies but is learning each day how to better control his thoughts and feelings. His achievements in sport, bearing in mind his road of the past two decades, proves that even under mental duress, an athlete can still achieve their dreams.

CAREER RECORD

International Achievements – World Title Medals

2022 World Champion of Champions Singles BRONZE Medal

2019 World Champion of Champions Singles GOLD Medal

2018 World Champion of Champions Singles BRONZE Medal

International Representation

Australian Emerging Squad 2018/2019

Australian Representative #132 (One representative match)

Australian Squad 2008-20111

Australian Under 25 Representative v New Zealand 2006 & 2007 (12 representative matches)

National Level Gold Medals / National Championships (20)

2023 Australian Sides Championship GOLD Medal (1)

2023 Australian Sides Championship Rink GOLD Medal (1)

2023 Australian Champion of Champions Singles GOLD Medal (4)

2021 Australian Champion of Champions Singles GOLD Medal (3)

2020 Australian Pairs GOLD Medal (1)

2019 Australian Fours GOLD Medal (1)

2018 Australian Champion of Champions Singles GOLD Medal (2)

2018 Victorian Open Singles GOLD Medal (1)

2017 Australian Champion of Champions GOLD Medal (1)

2017 Victorian Open VIC MEDAL (1)

2017 Australian Masters Games Pairs GOLD Medal (1)

2017 Australian Masters Games Triples GOLD Medal (1)

2017 Victorian Open Triples GOLD Medal (1)

2017 Victorian Open Mixed Pairs GOLD Medal (2)

2016 Victorian Open Pairs GOLD Medal (2)

2012 Victorian Open Pairs GOLD Medal (1)

2012 Victorian Open Mixed Pairs GOLD Medal (1)

2011 Australian Open Pairs GOLD Medal (1)

2009 Queensland Open Triples GOLD Medal (1)

2006 Victorian Grand Prix Triples GOLD Medal (1)

State Championships (26)

2023 New South Wales Champion of Champions Singles GOLD Medal (8)

2023 New South Wales Champion of Champions Pairs GOLD Medal (1)

2023 New South Wales One Grade State Pennant GOLD Medal (2)

2021 New South Wales State Interzone GOLD Medal (1)

2021 Victorian Champion of Champions Singles GOLD Medal (7)

2020 Victorian Singles GOLD Medal (3)

2020 Victorian Pairs GOLD Medal (3)

2019 Tasmanian Fours GOLD Medal (2)

2018 Tasmanian Singles GOLD Medal (2)

2018 Tasmanian Champion of Champions Singles GOLD Medal (6)

2018 Tasmanian Triples GOLD Medal (2)

2017 Tasmanian Triples GOLD Medal (1)

2017 Tasmanian Champion of Champions Singles GOLD Medal (5)

2016 Tasmanian Pairs GOLD Medal (2)

2016 Tasmanian Fours GOLD Medal (1)

2013 Victorian Champion of Champions Singles GOLD Medal (4)

2011 Victorian Champion of Champions Singles GOLD Medal (3)

2011 Victorian Singles GOLD Medal (1)

2009 Victorian Champion of Champions Singles GOLD Medal (2)

2008 Victorian Champion of Champions Singles GOLD Medal (1)

2007 Victorian Pairs GOLD Medal (1)

2006 Victorian Under 30 Singles GOLD Medal (3)

2003 Victorian Under 30 Singles GOLD Medal (2)

2001 Victorian Under 30 Singles GOLD Medal (1)

2000 Victorian State Pennant GOLD Medal (1)

1997 VSSSA Secondary Schools Fours GOLD Medal (1)

State Representative Test Matches (330)

New South Wales Squad – 2022 – current (28)

Tasmanian Squad 2014 – 2019 (91)

Victorian Squad 2004 – 2013 (206); 2020 (5)

Regional / Zone Championships (49)

Singles (7) 2021, 2020, 2018, 2017, 2015, 2014 & 2011

Champion of Champions Singles (9) 2021, 2018, 2017, 2013, 2011, 2009, 2008, 2006 & 2004

Under 30 Singles (7) 2008, 2007, 2006, 2005, 2004, 2003 & 2001

Pairs (10) 2020, 2018, 2015, 2011, 2008, 2006, 2005, 2004, 2002 & 2001

Mixed Pairs (1) 2020

Triples (8) 2021, 2016, 2015, 2008, 2007, 2006, 2005 & 2004

Fours (6) 2023, 2022, 2018, 2015, 2011 & 2010

Champion of Champions Fours (1) 2023

Club Championships (66)

Singles (15) 2023, 2021, 2019, 2018, 2017, 2016, 2013, 2012, 2011, 2009, 2008, 2007, 2006, 2004 & 2002

Pairs (14) 2023, 2020, 2019, 2018, 2017, 2016, 2015, 2014 (twice), 2012, 2010, 2009, 2008 & 2005

Mixed Pairs (2) 1996, 2007

Triples (12) 2023, 2019, 2017, 2016, 2015, 2011, 2010, 2006, 2005, 2004, 2002 & 2001

Fours (13) 2023, 2019, 2018, 2017, 2016, 2015, 2014, 2012, 2010, 2009, 2008 2004 & 2003

Major/Minor Pairs (1) 2016

21 Up, 100 Up, 2 bowl singles (9) from 1999-2007

Total: 162 titles at World, National, State, Regional & Club level

www.ingramcontent.com/pod-product-compliance
Lightning Source LLC
Chambersburg PA
CBHW071854290426
44110CB00013B/1142